HUSTLE YOUR WAY TO FINANCIAL FREEDOM

UNLEASH YOUR INNER SHARK

Tracey Pennywell & George Lynch

Published in United States of America

First Printing Edition, 2023

Table of Contents

INTRODUCTION

Ever wondered why some people seem to have a magical touch with money, turning every dollar into a cascade of wealth, while others struggle paycheck to paycheck, drowning in debt?

There's a valid reason for that.

The truth is that most of us were simply taught the wrong things about money. We were taught that concepts like investing and consulting a financial advisor are only for the rich. What our parents, caregivers, teachers, and elders failed to recognize was that those two concepts (amongst many others) come before wealth...not after it.

Money has become some mystical and elusive thing that seems so far out of reach for so many people. But the reality is that anyone can make money. The gross domestic product (the economy size) of all the countries in the world comes to a combined total of $142 trillion. Yes, TRILLION. To break that down into simple math for you, that's enough to buy 23 trillion supersized Big Mac Meals or 2,963 meals for every single person on Earth. That's the equivalent of 1 Big Mac Meal per person per day...for the next 8 years. Of course, the last thing we want is for any of you to be living on fast food for the next 8 years, but you get the picture: there's more than enough money in the world.

We can agree on that much.

The real problem is the hoarding of wealth on one end of the spectrum and the belief that we cannot make more than what we're already making. Again, this simply isn't true and we're going to crack that little nugget of non-truth wide open.

Brace yourself, because what you're about to discover will shatter every misconception you've ever had about money and wealth-building

The Future is Yours

Not more than two decades ago, we were at the mercy of others. It was either we were taught something in school, heard it from someone in the family, or stumbled across certain information. Having access to this wealth of knowledge (pun completely untended) around wealth building is something incredibly new to throngs of us around the world.

But that's a good thing.

That means that the gatekeepers can no longer keep countless people down. It also means that you have the opportunity to have financial freedom within the next decade (or sooner)!

Picture this: You, fully embracing your inner entrepreneur – unleashing your potential and stepping into a world where your dreams have no limits. You have the freedom to go where you want with whomever you want. You have the resources to explore the world with the people you care about.

But your journey isn't just about making money. It's about cultivating the millionaire mindset — the one that turns those dreams into a living, breathing, thriving reality.

The Time is Now

If you've ever wondered how to turn your financial life around, secure a future filled with abundance, and rewrite your destiny, you're in the right place. In this book, we'll be your guides through the forest of confusing concepts. We'll be your mentors and your friends on this journey to financial empowerment, budgeting brilliance, and creditworthiness mastery.

Now, here's the thing: We won't just throw numbers, jargon, and complex theories at you. We'll keep it real and relatable because we've walked the walk. We know exactly what it takes to build wealth from the ground up and utilize every resource at our disposal.

We'll dive into the core concepts that underpin the path to financial freedom. We'll break it down, step by step – from understanding the power of financial literacy to the undeniable cost of financial ignorance. We'll explore the art of crushing it with strong financial foundations, building your credit like a boss, and unraveling the secrets of successful investing. Ultimately, we'll go beyond the confines of what you can do with your own hard-earned cash and tap into the true power of Other People's Money (OPM). You'll see why developing multiple streams of income isn't just a smart move—it's a lifeline to long-term financial security.

By the end of this book, you'll be armed with the knowledge and tools to hustle your way to financial freedom. You'll be ready to unleash your inner shark and swim in the waters of success. At the end of the day, you'll become the embodiment of the saying "The world is your oyster".

It's time for you to grab your chance and hustle on.

So, are you ready?

Then, let's dive in!

TRACEY PENNYWELL & GEORGE LYNCH

Hustle Your Way to Financial Freedom: Unleash Your Inner Shark

CHAPTER 1 – THE POWER OF FINANCIAL LITERACY AND GENERATIONAL WEALTH

How many times have we seen entrepreneurs, star athletes, and even celebrities file for bankruptcy? How many times have we seen incredible businesses, with so much potential, fall to ruin? We'll tell you one thing for free – it has happened too many times for us to count. That's because, without financial literacy, you'll never have the discernment to keep your wealth and multiply it.

Just take Iron Mike as an example. The former heavyweight boxing champion, at one point one of the highest-paid athletes in the world, filed for bankruptcy in 2003. [1] According to financial experts, his extravagant lifestyle and a series of legal troubles contributed to his financial downfall. The good news is that he was able to build his wealth back, but that isn't the case for everyone who loses their fortune. What's more, without understanding the complexities of building wealth, gaining it all back can prove to be more difficult than initially earning it was.

The fact is that there isn't one magic solution to building and maintaining wealth. It isn't like some last-second trick shot that wins the entire game. It takes an orchestrated and concerted effort for you to not only increase your income but to keep it rolling in without you having to constantly be on guard. This road to financial freedom, however, starts with knowledge.

Chapter 1

The Road to Financial Freedom Starts with Knowledge

At the risk of sounding cliché, we have to stay right off the bat that the road to financial freedom starts with knowledge. You might be wondering why bother with financial education in the first place, right? Well, the short answer is that it's like having a superpower when it comes to handling your money. So, let's unpack why it's absolutely essential to get yourself a solid financial education.

First off, let's face facts — money matters. It's not just about having enough to cover your bills or splurging on a vacation. Money is tied to every aspect of your life – from your everyday decisions to your long-term goals. Having a grip on your finances means having control over your life. More importantly, new studies show that having enough money for all of your living expenses plus your goals can actually help you live a more enlightened life. This is because when you're in the throes of desperately trying to survive, you live a life operating from the instinct-driven side of your brain. [2]

You read that right. Financial struggle robs you of the ability to think rationally. It robs your children of stable, calm parents. It robs you of yourself. Your decision-making skills are weakened and you'll find yourself living with a scarcity mindset. For anyone who says money doesn't buy happiness, we'd like to ask them what their definition of happiness is. Because while money can't fix your problems, it can give you the time and space to come up with solutions to those problems.

If you're struggling with your health, money gets you access to specialists and a gym membership. If you're struggling with your mental health, money gets you access to therapists and mindset coaches. This is why being financially literate is such a game-changer.

Other than helping you build wealth; financial literacy also ensures that costly mistakes are avoided. Imagine you're driving a car, and you've never taken a driving lesson or read the manual. You're bound to make some costly mistakes, right? Well, money is like that car and your financial education is your driving lesson. It teaches you how to handle money responsibly and avoid those expensive potholes.

Just like small, everyday financial decisions, big ones like buying a house or investing in a business become a tightrope act without a financial education. You're basically throwing darts blindfolded. With the right knowledge, you can make informed choices that align with your goals and set you up for success.

Now, here's the fun part. Financial education isn't just about managing your money. As mentioned, it's also about growing it. It's like planting seeds in a garden and watching them turn into a lush, money-filled paradise. Learning about investing, saving smartly, and making your money work for you will help you avoid debt traps. Speaking of which, let's talk about the "D" word. It can be a nasty opponent if you don't know the rules of the game. Financial literacy helps you understand how debt works, how to manage it, and, most importantly, how to avoid getting trapped in a cycle of never-ending payments. After all, debt isn't all bad. When used correctly – as we'll discuss later on – you can actually leverage it to build the life of your dreams.

As you sit reading this book, you've most likely had a number of obstacles get in the way of your aspirations. Even if you've leveled up, you're not in the big leagues as you had hoped you would be by now. We can safely assume that much or you wouldn't be reading this right now. The truth is that the ceilings we place above ourselves are all fictional. There is no such thing as a limit to what you can achieve. We've only taught ourselves this because of the number of curveballs that life tends to throw our way.

But life loves throwing curveballs, like unexpected medical bills or car repairs, and it's not going to stop now. Knowing how to handle your money will give you the tools to handle these surprises without breaking a sweat. You'll have that emergency fund tucked away, ready to save the day. This can help you stay on track with those dreams and break through those ceilings.

Now, while we're on the subject and before we go any further, take a minute to think about your goals. What are your dreams – traveling the world, retiring early, starting a business, or buying a dream home? Whatever you dream of having, try to get to the root of the reason for it. More often than not, what we actually crave isn't the thing but what the thing can do for us.

For instance, having money means that you no longer need to struggle. Having a home, means you have somewhere safe to rest your head. Being able to travel, means that you get to do the one thing that the human soul craves – immerse itself in new experiences. Financial literacy is the roadmap that guides you toward those dreams. It shows you how to set goals and create a plan to turn them into reality. Not only that, but it shows you how to do it all without burning proverbial holes in your own pockets in the process.

This is important because, whether or not you have children of your own, having a long-term, future goal that you can work towards is important. Thinking about the legacy that you'll leave behind is a big piece of the puzzle. It's in our nature to live a life in service of others and that inherent nature is what drives us to create a legacy – no matter who benefits from it. Plus, when you're financially savvy, you can pass down your knowledge and wealth to future generations. You're not just securing your own future. You're setting up your family for success too.

So, there you have it. Having a financial education is like having a secret weapon in the game of life. It's about control – avoiding costly mistakes, making informed choices, growing your wealth, and so much more. So, don't sleep on it – let's get that financial education and unleash your money superpower!

Mastering the Basics of Financial Savvy

Alright, let's dive into the nitty-gritty of financial basics. This is where the rubber meets the road on your journey to financial freedom. We'll break down concepts like saving, compounding interest, investing, and developing that entrepreneurial mindset. Plus, we'll toss in a few extra nuggets of wisdom to get you on the right track. But let's start with saving money. For many of us, hearing about the importance of saving made us never want to save a cent in our lives. It wasn't so much the message but the tone in which the message was transmitted.

Here's the thing. Parents have good intentions and we can all respect our parents for facing the struggles of their time and managing to raise relatively well-rounded individuals. However – and this is a big **however** – their struggles were, as we just said, of *their time*. Money is different nowadays and, while some practices like saving still have merit, the way we go about it is different. It has to be – the financial landscape has changed! But we'll get into this a little later.

Either way, saving money isn't just a good idea. It's the foundation of your financial safety net. Think of it as your rainy-day fund, your "oh no, the car broke down" fund, or even your "someday I want to buy a house" fund. You can even set money aside for special occasions, unforeseen medical expenses, or just simple things like clothes. The point of saving is budgeting your money and telling it where to go. Of course, you need to have the means to save in the first place but, as we mentioned, we'll get into it later.

For now, let's brush over the 2 most common types of savings that you can have and why.

1. **Emergency Fund:** This is your first line of defense against unexpected expenses. Aim to stash away three to six months' worth of living expenses. It'll save you from resorting to credit cards when life throws you a curveball. Credit is important and relevant, but you have to know how to manage it.
2. **Short-Term Goals:** Saving isn't just about having something stashed for emergencies. It's also about achieving short-term goals. Maybe you want to take a vacation, buy a new laptop, or upgrade your car. Having a dedicated savings account for these goals keeps you on track.

But you have to know how saving works and the power of compound interest. This will also give you the upper hand where investing is concerned. So, what is it? Well, Einstein called compound interest the eighth wonder of the world and he was onto something. Compound interest is like a snowball rolling downhill — it starts small but grows into something massive over time. Basically, when you save or invest, you earn interest on your money. Over time, that interest earns interest of its own. It's like getting paid on your savings and the interest you've already earned. The longer your money compounds, the faster it grows. Here, you'll need to switch up your mindset and take yourself from thinking that time is against you to realizing that it's on your side. In fact, time is your best friend when it comes to compound interest. Starting your saving or investing journey early means your money has more time to grow. Even small contributions can turn into a sizeable nest egg.

Now, as we said, this isn't just for saving. Investing is a key component here and this is where you can truly see your money flourish. Keep in mind that investing isn't just for the rich or self-proclaimed finance whizzes. It's a powerful tool for growing your wealth over time. It all starts with something called "risk tolerance". Everyone has a different appetite for risk. Some people are comfortable with high-risk, high-reward investments, while others prefer safer, lower-return options. Your risk tolerance should align with your financial goals and timeline. In Chapter 5, we're going to help you figure out which end of the line you should be toeing.

The important thing to know right now is that you can't go putting all of your chips on the same table. That way, if one investment takes a hit, the others can help offset the loss.

To some degree, this requires you to develop an entrepreneurial mindset. Whether you're running your own business or not, adopting an entrepreneurial mindset can boost your financial success.

This includes prioritizing the following traits:

- **Grit and Resilience:** Entrepreneurs know that failure is part of the game. It's about dusting yourself off and coming back stronger. Don't be discouraged by setbacks. Use them as learning experiences.
- **Creativity and Innovation:** Thinking outside the box can lead to unique opportunities. Don't be afraid to explore new ideas, seek innovative solutions, and challenge the status quo.
- **Adaptability:** The business world is ever-changing and so is your financial life. Being adaptable and open to change is key. Embrace new technologies, stay informed, and be ready to pivot when necessary.

From there, managing your credit and ensuring that you're being "tax efficient" will take you to the height of the success that you've envisioned for yourself.

But we're getting a little ahead of ourselves. We've covered a lot of ground here and we hope that you understand that financial basics are the building blocks of your wealth journey. Saving, harnessing the power of compounding interest, investing wisely, and adopting an entrepreneurial mindset are keys to unlocking your financial potential.

There is one more element in our foundation-building that we need to touch on because of its level of importance in not only **making** you wealthy but also **keeping** you wealthy.

Let's talk a bit more about generational wealth and legacy building.

Generational Wealth: Building a Legacy That Lasts

So, you might be thinking, "Why should I care about building generational wealth when I don't have kids or don't plan on having any anytime soon?" Well, that's a good question and it's about time we dive into this topic. Before that, we want to assure anyone who already has children – even teenagers or young adult children – that it's not too late to talk about this, so this one is for all of you too.

First things first, let's clear up what we mean by "generational wealth." It's not just about passing on a big pile of money to your kids. It's about creating a legacy of financial knowledge, resources, and opportunities that benefit not only your children but also their children and generations beyond. Generational wealth is like a financial gift that keeps on giving – a ripple effect of prosperity that can touch countless lives. And here's why you should care about it, even if you're not planning to start a family anytime soon.

For one thing, when you focus on creating lasting financial stability and security, you're setting yourself up for a more comfortable and stress-free life in the present. Being able to put yourself in the mindset of having someone to leave something behind for will have you creating masses of wealth. What's even more awesome about this entire process is that – even if you don't have children of your own – you can set up a trust or charitable fund that will benefit from your financial wealth when you're gone.

When all is said and done, you'll be giving yourself the gift of purpose.

Next on the agenda is financial security. As you accumulate assets and savings, you'll have a safety net for life's unexpected curveballs. It's peace of mind knowing you can handle emergencies without having to scratch your head and wonder where you're going to get the cash from. But you already know this basic principle from earlier in this chapter. However, what we haven't unpacked is the fact that generational wealth can also enable you to retire earlier and enjoy life to the fullest while you're still young and spry. Not only that, but the financial freedom that comes from accruing generational wealth lets you pursue your passions. Plus, even without children, you can make a significant impact on your extended family, community, or causes that you're passionate about.

We haven't met a single person whose parents struggled and who didn't want to help them experience life's greater pleasures. Save for the people who had strained relationships with their parents, we don't know anyone who doesn't want to buy their parents a new home, a fancy new whip, or an island getaway. Besides your parents, generational wealth allows you to support family members in need. Whether it's helping a sibling through a tough time or providing educational opportunities for nieces and nephews, your resources can uplift your entire family.

What better feeling could there be than being known as the cycle breaker in your family – the one who changed everything and elevated everyone to new heights?

Go on. We'll wait for the answer.

The answer is that there aren't many feelings that we can think of that are greater than that.

Then we look beyond family. Outside of them, you can use your wealth to contribute to your community. Investing in local businesses, supporting charities, or funding educational programs can have a lasting impact on the lives of others. If you're passionate about a particular cause, like education, healthcare, or the environment, generational wealth gives you the means to create a lasting legacy by supporting that cause through donations or establishing a foundation.

If you're feeling like this is all a bit daunting, know that what we said earlier still holds true. Generational wealth isn't just about money. It's about knowledge. When you prioritize financial education and responsibility, you can pass on valuable skills that can benefit your family and future generations. Yes, your knowledge can be your most significant asset. Educate your family members about budgeting, investing, and smart financial choices. This will equip them with the tools to succeed.

In turn, this can help you to provide your family with opportunities you might not have had – ultimately ensuring they start their financial journey from a stronger position. Finally, encouraging an entrepreneurial mindset can lead to the creation of family businesses and investments, thus, further building generational wealth. Your family can learn to not just manage money but also grow it!

With all of this in mind, though, there are some things that you need to be aware of when you commit to the game that you're about to play. The first is that the rules can change as soon as you set foot on the court. While you might not plan on having children now, circumstances can change. But even if they don't, building generational wealth ensures you're prepared for whatever life throws your way. Moreover, the rules of moneymaking itself can change and this is why it's important to develop the mindset of lifelong learner who is dedicated to honing their financial literacy.

When you think of it, generational wealth is a long-term commitment that secures your family's future, even if you don't have children now. And always remember, generational wealth can ensure that your loved ones enjoy a comfortable retirement, free from financial stress.

So, there you have it.

Building generational wealth isn't just about kids — it's about creating a legacy of financial strength, knowledge, and impact that extends far beyond your lifetime. It's about securing your present, making a difference in your community, and leaving a lasting mark on the world. Whether you have children or not, generational wealth is a journey worth embarking upon – for you and your community.

We'll say this before we move on to the next chapter. Honing your financial literacy will leave you feeling empowered. When you know the inner workings of banking systems, loans, credit, investments, and more, you will not shy away from challenges. More importantly, nobody is going to be able to make a fool out of you where your money is concerned. You'll rip that wool right off your eyes and fashion the next great invention out of it. In the end, whether you're hoping to brush up on your money mindfulness or you're hoping to go that entrepreneurial route, things are about to take a very interesting turn for you.

So, let's get to it.

CHAPTER 2 – THE COST OF FINANCIAL IGNORANCE: BEING POOR IS EXTREMELY EXPENSIVE

The cost of being financially ignorant: a subject that is going to undoubtedly ruffle a few feathers and get a few more feeling amped up. Before you think we're here to judge or look down on anyone by using the word "ignorant", please know that this is the last thing we're trying to do. Let's break it down – to be ignorant is to lack proficiency or knowledge in certain areas. There are things that even we, as authors, are ignorant about.

To cut a long story short, it's impossible to know everything all at once.

However, financial ignorance can cost you your life and your freedom. This is why we want you to be as financially literate as possible. But we understand that some of you might be more motivated by the pitfalls of being financially ignorant than the benefits that we looked at in the previous chapter.

With this in mind, we're going to be delving into the financial jungle as our first port of call. This will give you that comparative shot of the financial literacy landscape.

So, let's take a deep dive into that now.

Navigating the Financial Jungle: Ignorance vs. Empowerment

Alright, let's start unpacking that little lurking element that doesn't get as much attention as it should — the steep price of financial ignorance. Whether you're just starting your financial journey or you've been cruising along without a roadmap, understanding the cost of not knowing can help you see things with clarity. Without the right knowledge in place, you could suffer due to something we like to call "The Ignorance Tax".

Let's use another analogy here. You're on a road trip without a GPS, a map, or even road signs. You're driving blind and making guesses at every turn – hoping that you'll eventually reach your destination.

What do you think is going to happen?

You're going to have to stop for directions every once in a while, but there's no way of telling whether those directions are accurate or if you're being led on a wild goose chase. Even if they are accurate, are these directions taking you the long way and making you waste your time?

One thing is for sure: you're going to get lost along the way. You're going to burn through fuel and take twice as long to reach your destination. The sad reality is that this scenario isn't too far from what it's like when you lack financial knowledge. We said it before and we'll say it again. Financial ignorance is like paying an "ignorance tax" throughout your life. It's the extra cost you incur when you don't have the essential knowledge needed to make informed financial decisions.

The question is how can you tell if you're already paying the price of ignorance tax?

Let's count the ways, starting with high-interest loans. One of the most noticeable ways financial ignorance hits you in the wallet is through high-interest loans. If you're not savvy about interest rates, you might end up with credit cards, personal loans, or payday loans that charge exorbitant rates. These interest payments can eat up a significant portion of your income, making it harder to get ahead financially. You would be amazed how many people started their businesses with nothing but a laptop and a few dollars in the bank. Yes, that is still a real thing in 2023.

And no, we're not telling you to stop having a coffee when it suits you or cut out every shred of joy from your life. However, it is important that you cut back on non-essential interest-bearing accounts indiscriminately. If you don't, they'll bleed you dry.

Other than missing the opportunity to invest those funds elsewhere, you could miss the opportunity to invest altogether if you're financially illiterate. Investing isn't just for the rich because, as already discussed, financial markets offer opportunities for your money to grow over time thanks to the magic of compounding interest. But if you're not aware of these opportunities or are too scared to invest, you miss out on potential gains. Over the long term, these missed opportunities can translate into millions of dollars in losses.

This underinvestment can have a ripple effect on your retirement and that's one of the worst things you could do to your future self. Planning for retirement is a crucial aspect of financial literacy. Without proper knowledge, you might underestimate how much you need to save for retirement or make poor investment choices in your retirement accounts. This can result in a less comfortable retirement or the need to work longer than you'd like. This brings us back to Exhibit A: lack of knowledge around savings or a lack of a desire to save. Again, financial ignorance often leads to poor savings habits. Without understanding the importance of saving and budgeting, you might find yourself living paycheck to paycheck.

This is not to disrespect or discredit anyone who is struggling to make ends meet at the moment. The financial climate that we're all living through is intense, which is exactly why we're trying to reach as many people and help as many of you reach the basket and make that winning shot. If you can save anything at all, try to. If you can help it, try not to leave yourself vulnerable to emergencies where you'll be forced to rely on credit cards or loans.

This will ultimately set you up for failure because, if you're already not aware of how credit works or how to manage it wisely, you might end up with a low credit score. This can affect your ability to secure loans, rent an apartment, or even get a job in some cases. Yes, some employers will pull your credit history to see if you're trustworthy. This is especially true if your profession has anything to do with accounting, finance, banking, or asset management. Plus, this becomes a vicious cycle like a dog chasing its own tail because poor credit scores often lead to higher interest rates on loans, costing you more money in the long run.

Speaking of costs, financial ignorance can lead to impulsive spending habits. You might not have a clear budget or financial goals, which makes it easy to overspend and accumulate unnecessary debt. Impulse spending can derail your financial progress and hinder your ability to save and invest. Before you know it, you'll be dealing with the side effects of missed financial goals. And once you're in that desperate state of life and of mind, you'll be more vulnerable to scammers. Add to this the fact that financial scams and fraud are prevalent in the digital age. Ignorance about financial security and how to protect yourself can leave you vulnerable to scams that can wipe out your savings or compromise your personal information.

Finally, when you've been put through the wringer and you're on your last, you'll find yourself dealing with incomparable stress levels. Money, after all, gives us the ability to survive and we're creatures that are bent on survival. This is why financial stress can take a toll on your mental and physical health. Ignorance about budgeting, debt management, and financial planning can lead to chronic stress, anxiety, and even depression. While money can't eradicate depression, it can give you the means and the tools to do something about it.

Financial ignorance can keep you stuck in a cycle of debt, prevent you from achieving your goals, and limit your financial freedom. It's like navigating through life with a blindfold on, hoping you'll stumble upon success. In the grand scheme of things, the cost of financial ignorance is high, not only in terms of money but also in the opportunities and dreams it can hinder. It's a tax that weighs you down, preventing you from reaching your full financial potential.

But it doesn't have to be this way.

Here's how you can avoid the total knockout of high-interest rates and poor decisions.

The TKO of High-Interest Rates and Poor Decisions

Let's talk about a financial pitfall that can quietly erode your wealth, hinder your financial progress, and (in the worst cases) ruin lives for years to come. We're diving deep into the world of high-interest loans and how they can take a significant bite out of your take-home income, potentially making you poorer than you actually are. We know that we touched on this in the previous subchapter, but there is so much more to get into.

That said, let's pick up where we left off with the idea of high-interest loans being like a dog that chases its own tail. These loans, whether they're in the form of credit cards, payday loans, or high-rate personal loans, might seem like a quick fix when you're in a financial pinch. Let's look into this further and say, for example, that you take out a $1,000 payday loan with a 400% annual interest rate (not uncommon). If you can't pay it off quickly (2-3 weeks), the interest piles up fast. In just two weeks, you could owe $1,400. In a month, $1,600. It's a slippery slope. [3]

We won't tell you what you could be doing with that money (yet), but we will tell you that the take-home hit is almost too much for anyone to shoulder on their own. If it isn't payday loans, it's personal loans and these can swallow up just as significant a portion of your paycheck as other high-interest loans. When it comes down to it, this will leave you with less money to cover essential expenses, let alone save or invest.

To make matters worse, high-interest loans can create the illusion of poverty even if your income is decent. Here's how it happens. First, you enter survival mode. When you're scraping by, unable to build savings or invest in your future, this can have you feeling trapped and alone. Despite the fact that so many people might be feeling the way you are, you'll feel like a failure and isolation will take root pretty quickly. This is because, when we're in survival mode, our minds lean towards negativity. In fact, it almost becomes our go-to and, more often than not, it's just our brain's way of keeping us safe from trying anything else that could potentially jeopardize our survivability.

With time, you'll lose sight of your dreams and all hope of the idea that they could become a reality. This lack of financial progress will keep you stuck in a rut and prevent you from making strides toward financial security. As for long-term goals – they'll become non-existent in this game of financial cat and mouse.

But it doesn't stop there.

Because we become so desperate to get out of the previous debt, we trick ourselves into thinking that another high-interest loan will do the trick. If we can just borrow enough to cover all of the other credit we've taken, we can focus on paying back just one loan, right?

Well, that depends. If the loan isn't high interest and it will help you amalgamate your debt so that you can actually get out of it, great! If it's high interest and will keep you trapped in a perpetual debt cycle, forget it. You'd be better off sitting down with each of the lenders you owe and negotiating lower rates or longer repayment terms. (Yes, you can do that.)

Keep in mind that interest on debt can compound like interest on investment. The more you borrow, the more you're likely to snowball that debt into something completely unmanageable. To exacerbate the situation, the damage doesn't stop at your take-home pay and immediate financial situation. High-interest loans have a ripple effect that can lead to a host of other problems.

What problems – you might ask?

Let's find out:

- **Missed Payments:** When a significant chunk of your income goes to loan payments, it's easy to miss other financial obligations like rent, utilities, or insurance premiums. This can result in late fees, damaged credit, utility disconnection, or even eviction.
- **Increased Stress:** Financial stress is a silent killer. Constantly worrying about how to make ends meet can take a toll on your mental and physical health. It's not that it *might* impact your overall well-being, it's guaranteed.
- **Limited Financial Options:** The weight of high-interest loans can limit your financial choices. You might have to turn down opportunities or forego investments that could have improved your financial outlook.
- **Damaged Credit:** Late payments and excessive debt can tank your credit score. A poor credit score can make it harder to secure affordable loans in the future, such as mortgages or car loans.

So, how do you break free from this?

Well, thankfully this is what this book is all about. Not only are we going to show you how to break free, but we're also going to help you pave the way for better financial decisions. The first order of business on your financial freedom agenda is budgeting. Start by creating a budget that accounts for your income, expenses, and debt payments. This will give you a clear picture of your financial situation. Also, when you budget down to the last penny (we're talking setting aside a budget for EVERYTHING), you might find that you're not as cash-strapped as you thought you were. It feels a whole lot better to have a single dollar bill to your name after all your bills than being under the assumption that you're actually over budget every month.

From there, you need to come up with a debt repayment plan. Prioritize paying off high-interest loans as quickly as possible. To do this, write down every single one of your debts, but don't put them in order of how much you owe. Put them in order of their impact on your life. For instance, **if you owe a bank $20,000 with an interest rate of 11% and you owe an unofficial lender $30,000 with no interest, pay the bank first.** We say this because interest of any kind – whether it's high or not, can keep you trapped in a cycle of debt. The faster you pay off accounts that bear interest, the faster you'll get out of debt.

So, we would recommend, negotiating with the unofficial lender. Get your payment down as low as possible and focus all of your efforts and excess funds into that bank loan. Yes, it's not going to pay off immediately, but it will get you out of debt faster. Then, once the bank loan is cleared up, plow all of the excess funds you were putting toward the bank loan into the unofficial loan. This will help you get out of debt faster.

There is another method that works really well in this scenario, but we'll touch on that in the next chapter.

Other than all of this, try to make lifestyle adjustments to curb expenses. If you're drowning in debt, consider seeking help from credit counseling agencies or debt relief programs. They can provide guidance and strategies to tackle your debt.

The important thing to acknowledge and to always stay aware of is the fact that high-interest loans are more than just a financial burden. They're a trap that can lead to a pile-up of financial problems. By taking control of your finances, budgeting wisely, creating an emergency fund, and seeking help when needed, you can escape the clutches of high-interest loans. It's a journey toward financial freedom, security, and peace of mind. To help keep you from getting caught up in a scrimmage that will have you fumbling the ball, let's talk credit.

Credit: The Potential to Destroy Lives

There's often a bit of mystique in the credit game, but credit is a tool that is often underestimated. It's not just a fancy plastic card or some random number. It's like your financial cred and it plays a massive role in your money journey. We don't want you to take this as your introduction to Chapter 4, so we'll be leaning more toward how credit can cause chaos in your life.

For starters, if you're not using credit correctly, it's going to hurt your credit score more than it helps it. The truth is that none of us get a base credit score to start off with. We all start at zero and our profiles are all assessed for risk before we get our very first line of credit. Once you have that credit card, if you go straight to maxing it out or underperform in terms of repayments, you're going to run into trouble. You might not even get any type of warning from your credit card provider that you're on dangerous ground. For most people, the only moment that serves as a wake-up call regarding their credit is the moment that they apply for their next line of credit – like a mortgage. Suddenly, they realize that all of those "it's only 1 day late" moments have added up to big losses in terms of their credibility.

Overall, credit often gets a bad rap because of some common misunderstandings like these. So, we're going to break down these myths and set the record straight. Let's start with the first breadcrumb that we left for you above: high utilization. People sometimes think that maxing out credit cards shows they're great with money. Nope! High credit card balances can actually tank your credit score.

Now, when people realize this, they often panic and try to pay off the card as quickly as possible and then close it. But this is another biggie. The belief that closing credit card accounts is a smart move might seem like a good idea, but – spoiler alert – it's not. You'd be better off getting your credit card down to a low balance and paying something towards it every month. This will give you a long and stable credit history with a balanced credit score. Rule of thumb: don't close accounts, especially if those accounts have a long history or low balances.

Yes, length matters. Credit history isn't just about how many years you've been on the face of this earth. It's about how long you've had credit accounts open. Having a short history can be a roadblock to accessing future lines of credit. Equally important is credit diversity. Focusing on just one type of credit, like credit cards, might seem like a good idea, but lenders like to see a mix of credit types, so being a one-trick pony can actually come back and bite you later.

Then we have another widespread fallacy. Some folks think avoiding credit altogether is a safe bet. But having no credit history can be like having no résumé for a job. In the end, you'll find it tough to get approved for loans, to rent an apartment, or even get shortlisted for some jobs.

Finally, we have the risk of forced account closure. Managing credit can be a tough nut to crack for us, so just imagine what it must be like for lenders. They have hundreds (if not, thousands) of accounts to manage and this can be a time-consuming, costly pursuit. The only way that they get anything out of it is if you're using your credit card and paying them interest. If your account sits idle, they might be losing more than their making off the monthly service fees. More importantly, if you have a bank-attached credit card with no additional service fees, they're not getting anything out of having to manage your credit account at all. In fact, they might be at risk (as are you) of falling prey to fraudsters.

So, they'll close your account for you.

While this is rare, it's important to find out what the limitations are around your credit card. Figure out how long you can keep the card without using it before the lender closes the account. That way, you'll know when and how to use your card. With that said, though, it's far easier to just use a couple bucks on the card each month to keep it active and to build your credit score.

Being financially ignorant in this regard will have you making bad decisions about your credit usage and how you operate your accounts. Trust us, you don't want to do that to yourself.

Now, let's keep this momentum going with strong financial foundations.

CHAPTER 3 – CRUSHING IT WITH STRONG FINANCIAL FOUNDATIONS

Having a strong financial foundation is enough to take you from barely getting by to being a billionaire on the fly. Throughout history, there have been countless examples of people who have beat the odds and have gone on to become incredibly wealthy. We idolize these people – we ask them what their secrets are – when in actuality, all that they've done is:

1. Educate themselves, and,
2. Remain consistent in their pursuits.

When you tell yourself that the only way is up, nothing can stand in your way. It is not a cliché. It is the simple truth. We possess more power than we can imagine, but the fear of being homeless or of losing a job (or any other money-rooted fear for that matter) keeps us stuck. If you want to make an impact on those around you and completely change the dynamics of your life, you need to get serious about believing in yourself. Because there isn't a single person on God's green earth that has anything special inside of them that you don't have. There is no secret sauce that they have, which has magically taken them from poverty to wealth.

It's all in the power of our minds.

Take Oprah Winfrey. Born into poverty in rural Mississippi, Oprah is now a media mogul, billionaire, and philanthropist. She overcame a challenging upbringing to become one of the most influential women in the world, primarily through her talk show and media empire. Then there's Ralph Lauren. The fashion icon (born Ralph Lifshitz in the Bronx) started with a modest necktie business. He went on to build the Ralph Lauren Corporation, which is now a global fashion empire. Finally, we have Jan Koum. The co-founder of WhatsApp was born in Ukraine and grew up in a small, cramped apartment. He eventually moved to the United States and created WhatsApp, which was later acquired by Facebook for billions of dollars.

None of these people have anything that you don't have.

OK. There is, perhaps, one tool these people used to make progress: the understanding that with no guts, there can be no glory.

No Guts, No Glory: Creating a Solid Money Mindset

Let's dive into a topic that's as essential as budgeting or investing but often gets overlooked: the money mindset. It's like the secret sauce that can make or break your financial journey. We're going to explore why many of us struggle with a scarcity mindset, how it's rooted in what we heard as kids, and why developing an abundance mindset is the real game-changer.

Let's start with the scarcity mindset. Before we go down this road, we just want to emphatically state that we have nothing but respect for parents who have struggled to get by. We have nothing but respect for those who are struggling today and we will continue to have respect for those who might struggle tomorrow. That said, there are ways that a struggling parent will word things that will have a negative effect on the way their children view money. Picture this: you're a kid, and you ask for something you really want. Maybe it's a new toy, a trip to an amusement park, or even just an allowance. You're immediately met with: "Money doesn't grow on trees," "We can't afford that," or "That's rich folk stuff. It's like a broken record, playing over and over in your head.

This is how a scarcity mindset often takes root.

But what could be said differently? If there's no money, there's no money, right? Nothing can change that.

That's where we've all been wrong for the longest time. There is something that can be said differently. Instead of "We can't afford that," we could transition to "We can't afford that yet." The power of yet gives a child the idea that, with time, they might be able to afford something. This then sows the seed of hope in a child's mind.

However, we're not here to discuss child psychology. We're just simply pointing out where your scarcity mindset might stem from and where you get the idea that wealth is for "them" or "others". Ultimately, as kids, we're like sponges – just soaking up everything around us. The messages we heard about money, whether from our parents, teachers, or peers, shaped our beliefs and attitudes. When we heard phrases like "money is tight" or "we can't have it all", it was like planting seeds of scarcity in our minds. This grows into a mindset where we believe there's never enough. It's like living life with a constant fear of running out and it can impact everything from our spending habits to our financial goals.

What's strange, though, is that it can make you spend more. This isn't true for everyone, but hear us out. When you have a scarcity mindset, you constantly feel like the money will run out eventually. Because of that thought, you go around buying everything you think you need. You buy everything you wish you had growing up and you try to hoard material items in a bid to build this false cushion of perceived wealth around you. Again, this isn't true for everyone nor is this a hard fact. This is merely something that we've both observed and, if this resonates with you, know that you're on the verge of letting a scarcity mindset control your life.

That fear, which a scarcity mindset is rooted in, can drive a person insane. The fear of not having enough, the fear of making the wrong financial choices, and the fear of the future can lead you down some pretty negative financial rabbit holes. It's like a cloud that hangs over our financial decisions and sways them without any control on your part. That feeling of helplessness – of being out of control can be paralyzing.

So, how do we break free from this scarcity cycle?

It starts with recognizing that the scarcity mindset is a construct that we can deconstruct and rebuild [4]. First, you'll need to understand that the messages you heard as a child weren't your fault. They were shaped by the beliefs and experiences of your parents and caregivers. But this is not about blaming anyone. It's about acknowledging the past to create a different future. Once you understand this and hold no resentment toward anyone for it, you can begin challenging negative beliefs. Start questioning those old beliefs. When you catch yourself thinking, "I can't afford it" or "there's never enough," challenge those thoughts. Are they based on facts or old narratives? Take it one step further and ask yourself, "What can I do to afford it?" You can also reframe your thoughts to, "Somehow, there is always enough for my needs."

Look, we're not saying if your possessions are being repossessed left and right that you should just sit there and focus on just thinking happy thoughts. What we are saying is that if you're moderately financially stable right now, there are things that you can do to alter your mind. When you alter your mind, you'll alter your future. Trust us when we say this. It really works!

On the topic of happy thoughts, try to cultivate a sense of gratitude for what you do have. Shifting your focus from what you lack to what you appreciate can be a powerful tool in changing your mindset. This is because a negative mind will always seek out problems to solutions whereas a positive mindset will seek out solutions to problems. When you practice gratitude in your everyday life, you'll be able to see through the noise – through the Instagram feed noise and Facebook reel chaos – to find opportunities. Ideas will come to you via the information that you're inundated with every day. Instead of seeing things through a fearful, scarcity-induced lens, you'll see them with a lens of hope.

It's at this time when you can truly begin to visualize abundance. You don't have to while away the hours dreaming of that all-new Benz in your driveway, but just practice visualization techniques where you see yourself achieving your financial goals. When you can envision yourself living an abundant life. It's like planting new seeds of possibility in your mind.

This will all help you shift into an abundance mindset. It's like a mental switch that flips from "not enough" to "more than enough". With an abundance mindset, you see opportunities where others see obstacles. It's like having a wide-open field of possibilities. You also make financial decisions from a place of confidence, not fear. It's like stepping into the financial unknown with a sense of adventure. What's crazier is the fact that many people believe (with some semblance of evidence in their own lives) that an abundance mindset can actually attract wealth and prosperity [5]. When you believe in abundance, you're more likely to take actions that lead to financial success. Not only that, but you'll also be able to bounce back from setbacks more easily. It's like having a rubber ball mentality — you may get knocked down, but you always bounce back.

There are a number of ways that you can step into this mindset, but we'll give you a few of the more common tips that seem to work for a wide variety of people:

- **Affirmations:** Use positive affirmations to rewire your thinking. Repeat phrases like "I am abundant" or "Money flows to me effortlessly" daily.
- **Surround Yourself:** Spend time with people who have an abundance mindset. Their positivity and outlook can be contagious.
- **Practice Generosity:** Share your wealth – whether it's your time, knowledge, or resources. Giving creates a sense of abundance and fulfillment.
- **Set Bold Goals:** Challenge yourself with ambitious financial goals. It's like telling the universe, "I'm ready for abundance".
- **Stay Curious:** Keep learning and exploring. The more you know, the more confident you become and the more abundance you can attract.

When the clock is up in this game called life, how do you want to say you spent it? In the grand scheme of things, your money mindset is the compass that guides your financial journey and helps you spend in the right way – literally and figuratively. If your mind is stuck in scarcity mode, you'll always feel like you're running on empty. But by acknowledging the past, challenging negative beliefs, and embracing the abundance mindset, you can flip the script. Remember, folks, abundance isn't just about money. It's a mindset that impacts every aspect of your life. So, dare to believe in abundance, visualize your financial goals, and watch as your mindset transforms your reality. With that positivity coursing through you, you can take a real stab at your budget and cut unnecessary expenses mercilessly.

Budgeting Like a Pro: A Strategy for Success

You might be thinking, "Budgets? Yawn." But trust us, this is the game-changer that'll give you the keys to your financial kingdom. We're going to explore why having a budget and a trusty spreadsheet is like having a GPS for your money, and why the zero-based budgeting approach is your golden ticket to financial freedom.

Before we do that, let's tie up a little loose end. In the previous chapter, we looked at how to pay off high-interest loans and credit. Now, we want to get into this in further detail. Your debts, after all, are a part of your monthly budget and can prevent you from cementing that financial foundation. For this, we turn to Dave Ramsey's snowball effect. For those of you who don't know who that is, we'll give you a brief introduction. Dave Ramsey is a renowned financial expert, author, and radio host. He is best known for his practical advice on budgeting, debt management, and personal finance. Ramsey's ***Total Money Makeover*** system has helped millions achieve financial success through sensible budgeting and debt reduction strategies. Now, not everything he says falls into the pile of advice that we agree on, but his snowball method is a lifesaver for anyone in debt. Here's what he and his team advise [6]:

1. Begin by arranging your debts in ascending order (from the smallest balance to the largest) without considering interest rates.

2. Ensure you meet the minimum payments for all your debts, except for the smallest one.

3. Allocate as much extra money as you can toward paying off the smallest debt.

4. Continue this process until each debt is completely paid off.

You can also take whatever you were paying toward the smallest debt and add it to the next smallest debt on the list once the first is paid off in full. It has a compounding effect and gets you to where you need to go that much quicker.

Doing this and sticking to a budget will set you up financially. You have to tell your money where to go and what to do because it is like a mischievous rogue that is constantly on the move. If you don't give it a mission, it'll go on secret missions of its own, disappearing without a trace. And guess what? Those rogue missions often lead to broke-ville.

This is what we like to call the curious case of the **Wandering Dollar**. But budgeting comes in as an effective antidote to this problem. A budget is like turning on the lights in a dark room. It illuminates where your money is coming from and where it's going. This means no more financial blind spots.

Simply put, without a budget, spending can spiral out of control. But with one, you decide how much goes into each spending category. It will also help you to align your spending with your financial goals.

Budgeting Challenge: Over the next 30 days, write down everything you spend – down to the last red cent. See how much you're spending in each pay cycle and where it is going. If you're always behind on card payments by $50 but you spend $200 on your nails

---

every month, there's a problem – and it's not that you don't have enough but that you're not prioritizing well enough.

Having a budget is important because when unexpected expenses pop up, a budget provides a safety net. You cannot have luxuries when you're not covering necessities. That's just putting the cart before the horse and then complaining that the horse won't budge. After you've paid your bills, pay yourself first and pay your emergency fund next. Then, you can look into additional spending. Just don't forget to factor in investing and entrepreneurship

At the end of your budgeting efforts, you should have zero dollars left over. This is known as the Zero-Based Budgeting Magic. This method ensures every dollar has a job, leaving no money to wander off into the financial wilderness. In other words, zero-based budgeting means every dollar you earn gets allocated to a specific category or purpose. Your income minus your expenses equals zero. With zero-based budgeting, you decide where your money goes, rather than letting it decide for you. Your essentials come first, followed by your goals, investments, and entrepreneurial dreams. This approach helps you eliminate waste in your spending. When every dollar is accounted for, you'll be less likely to splurge on things that don't align with your goals.

But keep this in mind: zero-based budgeting isn't about being rigid. It's about being intentional with your money. You don't have to have a complete meltdown if you go a little over budget in the first month or two. You can adjust your budget as your financial situation evolves. To get started, follow the simple steps below:

- **Know Your Income:** Start by understanding your income. This should include your salary, side hustle earnings, or any other sources of money.
- **List Your Expenses:** Make a comprehensive list of your monthly expenses. Categorize them into essentials (like rent and groceries), goals (like savings and investments), and dreams (like starting a business).
- **Allocate Your Funds:** For every dollar you earn, allocate it to one of your expense categories. Use a trusty spreadsheet or a budgeting app to keep track.
- **Monitor and Adjust:** Keep an eye on your budget regularly. If you notice overspending in one category, adjust it by pulling funds from another. But if this keeps happening, consider rearranging your budget.
- **Save and Invest:** As you gain control over your money, start diverting funds toward savings, investments, or entrepreneurial endeavors.

The bottom line is that budgeting isn't rooted in restricting your spending. The primary goal of any budget should be to empower you to make conscious financial decisions. When you tell your money where to go, you take charge of your financial destiny.

So, are you ready to take control of your financial future? Then, let's delve into rainy-day funds.

Rainy-Day Funds: Your Shield in Times of Need

This is where the financial battle is won and lost. When things are already tight (financially speaking), having nothing to go toward an emergency can leave you one bad day away from ruin. Let's face it, life has a way of throwing curveballs when you least expect them.

Your car breaks down, your roof starts leaking, or you face unexpected medical bills. These situations aren't just stressful; they can send your finances into a tailspin. That's where your rainy-day fund steps in as your financial guardian.

Look, you don't have to be saving hundreds of dollars every month. Even small contributions can set you on a path to financial resilience. Plus, knowing that you have a safety net can bring peace of mind and, as we learned earlier, your mentality and mindset are crucial. Not only can money help you live a stable life, but the lack thereof can impact your mental well-being.

To really drive this point home, let's paint a few real-life scenarios to illustrate just how important a rainy-day fund can be.

Scenario 1 – Medical Emergency:

Estimated Cost – Urgent Care: 200. ER: $1,300.

You or a family member falls ill, and medical bills start piling up. Without an emergency fund, you might be forced to choose between health and financial stability.

Scenario 2 – Car Trouble:

Estimated Cost – Major Car Service: $400. Repairs: $1,500.

Your car, your lifeline to work, breaks down unexpectedly. Repairs can be costly, and without savings, you're stuck scrambling for transportation.

Scenario 3 – Job Loss:

Estimated Cost – 1 Month at Home: $4,000. 3 Months: $12,000.

In an uncertain job market, even the most secure positions can become vulnerable. A rainy-day fund can provide a financial buffer during unemployment.

Scenario 4 – Home Repairs:

Estimated Cost – Minor Repairs: $390. Major Repairs: $8,000.

Your home is your sanctuary, but it's not immune to wear and tear. A leaking roof or a broken furnace can lead to significant expenses without savings.

Scenario 5 – Unexpected Travel:

Estimated Cost – $300+

Sometimes, life throws you a curveball that requires immediate travel, like attending a family emergency or a last-minute work trip. Your rainy-day fund can cover those unexpected costs.

As you can see, when life hands us lemons, we won't always have the tools to make lemonade. Having the money to buy those tools (in other words to pay unforeseen expenses) is important. Financial experts often recommend having at least three months' worth of living expenses stashed away in your rainy-day fund. This cushion can provide peace of mind during temporary setbacks, job losses, or medical emergencies.

We have to emphasize that financial circumstances vary widely and not everyone can quickly achieve a three-month fund. The key is to start saving, no matter how small the contributions might be. As we've said before, even setting aside as little as $5 or $10 a month can set the stage for positive financial habits. There's no shame in starting small. Everyone's financial journey is unique. The important thing is that you're building a safety net, no matter how slowly.

We're also aware that life circumstances can change and so can your ability to save. As your financial situation improves, you can gradually increase your contributions to your rainy-day fund.

To get it set up in the first place, this is what to keep in mind:

- **Set a Goal:** Determine how much you'd like to save in your rainy-day fund.
- **Set it & Forget it:** Set up automatic transfers from your checking account to a separate savings account designated for emergencies.
- **Use Windfalls:** Put unexpected windfalls like tax refunds, bonuses, or gifts directly into your rainy-day fund.

That's really all there is to it. In most cases, taking the first step is the scariest part of this transaction. Once you get into the habit of doing things differently, you'll be able to take on life's challenges and uncertainties. Remember that while having three months' worth of savings is a great goal, even small contributions can set a positive financial mindset in motion. So, start building your financial safety net today, knowing that you're taking an important step toward your vision. No one else is going to do it for you and you can see that as frightening or empowering.

Personally, we know that the right money mindset will look at that as empowering.

Now, let's dredge that bad credit up off the metaphoric ocean floor and clean it up.

CHAPTER 4 – THE CREDIT BLUEPRINT: RISE ABOVE THE REST

We've given you a sneak peek into credit mastery, but this is where we're going to provide you with a blueprint for success. This next chapter is going to have you punching a weight above the rest and taking home the gold in credit benefits and bonuses. Not only is this going to help you increase your credit score, but it's also going to net you some pretty sweet deals on future lines of credit as well as rewards that you can use right now.

Yes, there are people who get to travel the world for free by simply using their credit card for all of their purchases and paying it all back before the amount spent incurs any interest. That means, those who have $1,000 to spend on groceries this month, they'll put it on their card and pay it back within a week to avoid fees and interest. At the end of the year, they'll have cashback rewards, travel miles, and discounts on accommodation[1]*.

What we're trying to get at is this: credit cards aren't all that bad. If you're avoiding credit cards in a bid to keep your credit score stable and give you financial stability, you've got it all backward. Credit is the one way that you can get rewarded for spending.

Plus, the more diverse your mix of credit, the more likely you are to come off as a good risk for all lenders (and employers) in the future. So, let's start cracking into that credit wisdom.

---

[1] Dependent on what type of credit card you have and who your lender is.

Chapter 4

Credit Wisdom: Navigating the Maze of Financial Success

There are few things that are more important than getting your financial ducks in a row and having a paper trail to stand as a record of your credibility. We know that so many people fall prey to the old adage *"cash is king"*. However, if you don't have a credit history, you're tying your hands. You don't like the system? Yeah...who does? You think capitalism is tearing the world apart at the seams? We might agree with you in some respects. The fact is that whether you like it or not, this is the game that they're running. If you don't play by the rules and find a way to maximize your potential through the loopholes, you're going to be sidelined to the benches before the first whistle even blows.

So, we're going on this journey of building a good credit foundation and we're starting with your credit history. As we said before, try to think of credit history as your financial resume. It shows how you handle your debts. Without it, getting loans or good deals is like trying to enter a club with no ID — you won't get far. Plus, you already know that with good credit, you get the VIP treatment. This includes low interest rates, higher credit limits, and fancy credit cards with amazing rewards.

But your credit history isn't just necessary for living the high life via your rewards and travel points. It's also necessary for everyday life. If you're looking at making a move to a larger home in the burbs, for instance, credit scores become even more important. Strangely enough, not that many apartments in the cities are as tough on people with average credit, but if you want to level up your living quarters, that score better be on the higher end of the scale. Even certain utility companies run credit checks. Essentially, your credit history is your financial reputation and it can open doors to opportunities or slam them shut. Here's a brief snapshot of credit score ranges and how lenders – as well as landlords – regard them.

300-579	POOR
580-669	FAIR
670-739	GOOD
740-799	VERY GOOD
800-850	EXCELLENT

Table 1: Credit Score Ranges

You can get away with a credit score in the "fair" bracket, but not for very long. If you plan on keeping your life exactly the way it is, then don't do anything about your score. But if you want to start taking your dreams seriously, it's time to start doing what you can to pick that score up.

Here's the deal. Banks and lenders won't exactly roll out the red carpet to educate you on the ins and outs of credit. It's like a silent game where you're expected to know the rules, but no one hands you the rulebook. But you can write your own rulebook by taking your credit into your own hands. The best way to go about this is to have a look at your credit report to make sure everything is above board. If you don't know what a credit report is or where to find it, don't sweat it. We're not here to judge you. We're here to help.

Your credit report is a document that contains your credit history. It includes all of the hard inquiries that you've had on your account (flags when you apply for credit) as well as the history of missed and/or late payments for the last 24 months. When you apply for credit for the first time, you will get a credit score or Fair Isaac Corporation (FICO) score as well as the first dot on your credit report.

Depending on which institution provided the credit, this report will sit with:

- Experian,
- Equifax,
- TransUnion, or,
- Innovis.

In most cases, banks will report to all 3 of the major credit bureaus (the first 3 above), but it's important to find out if they report to Innovis and to keep track of that report.

Now, we have a question for you.

If you already know what all of this is and you've gone over your report recently, have you ever stopped to wonder about those inquiries on your credit report? Banks won't always tell you how to dispute them...even when they're inaccurate or questionable. But this is so important.

So, how do you dissect credit inquiries?

To answer that, let's start with a few credit-related definitions.

1. **Hard Inquiries:** These are typically made when you apply for credit, like a loan or a credit card. They can temporarily lower your credit score but should fall off after 2 years.

2. **Soft Inquiries:** These are more like background checks. They happen when lenders or companies check your credit for pre-approved offers, for employment purposes, or when you check your own credit. They don't affect your credit score.

3. **Disputing Inaccuracies:** If you spot inaccurate or unauthorized inquiries on your credit report, you have the right to dispute them. It's like cleaning up your credit report and ensuring it accurately reflects your financial history.

Now, here's the kicker. If the lender who is responsible for your hard inquiries or delayed payment reports cannot – without a shadow of a doubt – prove that you applied for the credit in question, they have to contact the relevant credit bureaus to have that information removed.

Other than being aware of your score and monitoring your report, you also need to be aware of the perks that are tied to your credit card. Many folks aren't even aware they signed up for fiscal insurance when they got their credit cards. And even if they did, they might not fully understand what it covers. In some cases, when you're unemployed and drowning in credit card debt, you might have an option to have the credit owed waived. That is particularly true if you signed up for credit insurance that covers unemployment due to disability or injury. But here's the catch — it can lead to account closures and potentially impact your credit score. Ultimately, only you can make the informed decision of whether to cash in that insurance (if you have it) or to keep trying to pay the debt down on top of being unemployed.

Nonetheless, for those of you who are interested in this aspect of credit insurance, we can let you in on what most policies cover. Your policy might include:

- Job loss,
- Disability,
- Long-term unemployment, or,
- Death.

Before tapping into fiscal insurance, run the numbers and evaluate your financial situation carefully. Consider the benefits of debt relief against the potential impact on your credit. But be honest with yourself. There is no point in holding on to hope only to sink yourself further into debt.

Now that you're armed with knowledge about credit inquiries and fiscal insurance, it's time to build your credit like a boss.

Building Credit Like a Boss: Unlocking Opportunities

Welcome to the big leagues, where credit isn't just a score—it's a strategy. Building credit like a pro is like mastering a skill that can open doors to financial freedom. We're diving deep into the world of credit management, from maintaining low credit card utilization to smart use of store credit – all while keeping your financial well-being at the forefront.

First up: the 25% utilization rule.

Typically you want to aim for that sweet spot between 20% and 30%. This means that, if your credit limit is $5,000, you only ever spend $1,250 (25%). However, landing somewhere around $1,000 (20%) and $1,500 (30%) is perfectly fine. You might be wondering why on earth you would have a $5,000 credit limit if you can't use it all, but in this game, you don't want to look desperate. If you come off as financially unstable, it will impact your score even if you make those payments on time every month.

To cut a long story short, your credit card utilization is the ratio of your credit card balances to your credit limits and it's important to stick to them. This will show lenders that you're responsible and not relying heavily on credit. It's like maintaining a good balance between using credit and managing your finances wisely.

But don't forget what we discussed in Chapter 2. While credit can be a powerful tool, it can also become a financial pitfall if you're not careful. Avoiding high-interest credit is like dodging a financial landmine.

Also, be aware of the fact that store credit is also reported to credit bureaus. Yes, folks, that Costco Anywhere Visa and Walmart Rewards™ Card are real credit cards and they get reported just like regular cards. That's good news and bad news because store credit can be a double-edged sword. It can help you build credit and provide financing options, but it can also tempt you to overspend.

As with any credit card, use store credit for necessary and planned purchases, not impulse buys. Treat it as a financial tool, not a shopping spree pass. Also, ensure you make payments on time. Late payments can hurt your credit score and the high interest rates on store credit make those missed payments even costlier. Finally, keep the card open. Store credit can contribute to a lengthy track record of good credit usage, which can positively impact your credit score over time.

If you can, try to commit to the Cash Rule, which states that you should only buy what you can afford using store credit (or any other form of credit for that matter). This is particularly important when you've just received a new credit card because it acts as a litmus test for responsible buying. So, as the rule goes, only buy something on a credit card if you can afford it in cash. This way, you'll be able to pay the card down quickly and keep it within the correct utilization range.

There are exceptions to this rule, like buying a car or property, but these generally can't be bought on your average credit card. For everyday expenses like clothing, accessories, or fancy furniture, don't go broke trying to buy on credit. If you can't afford it in cash or within a reasonable credit card balance, reconsider the purchase. This means learning to prioritize needs over wants.

Now, let's look at some other options for building and maintaining your credit. This is going to be a must for anyone who is starting their credit journey from scratch or trying to build back their rep after a bad credit stint.

Credit-Building Loans	These small installment loans are designed to help you build or rebuild credit. They're typically offered by credit unions or community banks.
Prepaid Credit Cards	These cards require you to deposit a certain amount of money as collateral. They function like regular credit cards but don't carry the risk of accumulating debt.

Table 2: Building & Maintaining Credit

Both options above can help establish a credit history if used responsibly. Make on-time payments and manage your finances wisely to maximize their credit-building benefits. Remember to keep an eye on your credit report (at least annually) to spot errors, unauthorized inquiries, or suspicious activity. If you find discrepancies on your credit report, dispute them as soon as possible with the credit reporting agencies.

Before you sign on that dotted line for new credit, review the terms and conditions of your credit card's fiscal insurance coverage. Know what it includes and under what circumstances it can be utilized. While unemployment can be a curveball, having a financial plan in place can help you navigate these challenging times without sacrificing your credit score. In this day and age, nothing is promised to any of us, so don't think you're indispensable at a job.

And don't forget that budget from Chapter 3!

Stay on top of your finances by creating a budget that ensures you meet your financial obligations – even during uncertain periods. Your credit is a powerful tool in your financial arsenal and it's up to you to use it wisely. While banks may not hand you a manual on credit management, you can take charge by understanding credit inquiries, disputing inaccuracies, and making informed decisions about fiscal insurance. Remember, your credit is like a financial fingerprint — it's unique to you and can shape your financial opportunities. So, stay vigilant, take control of your credit, and keep your financial doors open for whatever opportunities life brings your way.

If you can keep all of this in mind, you'll be on to a financial winning streak in no time. The awesome thing about this is that once you get that momentum – and the rush of seeing yourself succeed – you'll become practically unstoppable. Add the following hacks to that mix and you'll be set for life!

Hacks for Elevating Your Credit Score

Congratulations on leveling up your credit game! Now, it's time for you to explore some advanced strategies and hacks for improving and safeguarding your credit score like a true pro. These are the things that most lenders don't want you to know about. Listen up. It's not that they're insidious or that they want to see you fail. It's just that people have leveraged these tools in a way that – well – doesn't work in a bank's best interests.

Either way, we're here to help you, not corporations, so here's your first hack. It's called the credit freeze strategy and it goes a long way when your credit score is teetering on the edge of danger. If you find yourself on the verge between "FAIR" and "POOR", it's time to pull out the big guns and use a credit freeze. It's a security measure that restricts access to your credit report. Even if someone tries to apply for credit in your name, the lender won't be able to access your report, preventing fraudulent activity. Moreover, it prevents lenders from carrying out hard and soft inquiries without your consent.

To freeze your credit, you'll need to contact each of the three major credit bureaus to request a credit freeze. They'll provide you with a unique PIN for future access. Just remember that while a credit freeze is a powerful tool, it can also hinder your ability to apply for legitimate credit. When you're ready to apply for new credit, you'll need to unfreeze your credit temporarily.

The second hack that you can tap into is called the Credit Alert. Many credit monitoring services offer real-time alerts for changes to your credit report. These can help you stay on top of your financial reputation. If you've had any fraudulent activity on your account before and you're not in a position to freeze (or continue freezing) your credit, then this will be your lifeline. They act as an early warning system. They notify you of any significant activities on your credit reports, such as new credit inquiries, changes in account balances, or unfamiliar accounts being opened in your name. Detecting unauthorized or erroneous activities as fast as possible can help you take immediate action to fix the issues before they spiral into a disaster. Probably the best part of all of this is the power that alerts give you to maintain control over your credit profile. By staying informed about changes in your credit history, you can proactively manage your financial reputation, ensure accuracy, and work to improve your credit score. This can be particularly crucial when you're planning to apply for loans or credit in the future, as lenders rely heavily on your creditworthiness.

Plus, in today's digital age, where identity theft and credit fraud are on the rise, credit alerts will protect your financial well-being. If you're not already on the up about this, safeguarding your personal and financial information to prevent identity theft is vital. Use strong, unique passwords and consider using identity theft protection services. While you're on a credit-building journey, be cautious about applying for too much new credit at once. Multiple hard inquiries in a short period can hurt your score.

It might sound like work and you're right – it is. Building and protecting your credit score like a pro involves not only advanced strategies but also vigilance and smart financial practices. Utilize the power of a credit freeze when your score is at risk and consider credit-building loans or secured credit cards to strengthen your credit history. If you have anything to dispute, you can do this yourself with a simple letter of dispute or a phone call to any of the relevant credit bureaus.

- **Experian – 1-888-397-3742**
- **Equifax – 1-866-640-2273**
- **TransUnion – 1-833-806-1626**
- **Innovis – 1- 800-540-2505**

Using credit is the only way to build credit and that's the plain fact of the matter. But using credit regularly means that you have to use it wisely. Monitoring your credit reports and protecting your personal information are all essential aspects of maintaining a strong financial reputation. With these hacks and practices in your toolkit, you're well on your way to mastering your credit journey and achieving financial empowerment.

It's all about using your credit, paying it down, rinsing, and repeating. For many of us, the understanding of how credit works and how to use it efficiently was never something on the table. Schools aren't teaching this and many of our parents are still under the wrong impression where credit is concerned. If some of this information is new to you, you're not alone. Don't think about the "coulda, woulda, shoulda" of life. Yes, if you had known this sooner, you could have done something about it. But you know better now, so do something about it from today onward. When you get that credit report cleared up and you're steadily building your credit score, you can team it up with your investment hustle for maximum reward.

That's up next.

Chapter 5 – Investment Hustle: Raking in Wealth for the Long Haul

This is where things start to get really interesting. We're walking into the areas of your financial life where money is made. Now, there are a few hidden gems that can make all the difference on your investment journey, so it's important to consider them all when you're starting out. With that said, life is a process of learning on the go. Our job is to inspire you to get curious and to take action on your own.

This is something that we want to get a little deeper into because there are so many of you who think you need permission. This is particularly true if you were raised with sense. In fact, the more sensibly you were raised, the more prone you might be to coloring inside the lines. What you need to understand is that the lines move. You are now the captain of your own ship and you need to chart the course ahead.

Stop waiting for someone to come and tell you that it's ok to invest. More importantly, start understanding that your fear of failure is the fear of disappointing those around you or of not doing "what you were told". That's old news now. You're grown and you are the only person that you need to check in with. Your permission is the only one that matters. Of course, if you're married, check in with your spouse and go on a collaborative journey together.

However, always keep in mind that this journey is yours to take. If you really want to start raking in wealth using investment as your MO, you're going to need to get real with yourself. You'll need to understand what you can afford to risk and what you can't. You'll need to be honest about the type of lifestyle you want and why. From there, you can make your money work for you and use the magic of compound interest to reach the levels of success you envision for yourself.

Compound Interest Magic: Let Your Money Work for You

Compound interest – a topic that we've brought up several times at this point (and for good reason). That's because it's in the supercharged world of compound interest where your cash becomes a financial superhero. Buckle up because we're about to decode the magic behind compound interest to help you better understand why it's your ultimate money ally.

First and foremost, we'd be remiss not to demystify what compound interest actually is. While we've given you a simplified version of it, we'd like to help you really get to grips with what it can do for your financial well-being. Essentially, compound interest is the interest that keeps on giving. Working with compound interest means that you'll earn not just on your original stash but on the interest it has earned before. In other words, it's interest on top of interest!

The longer your money stays invested, the crazier compound interest becomes. Think of it as your money hopping in a time machine and bringing back bags of cash from the future. It's important that you stay realistic regarding how much you can invest and how frequently because this will determine whether or not you can reach your ultimate financial goals. But before we drone on about what we've already discussed, let's work on some hypothetical facts and figures. Using these made-up numbers, we'll illustrate the power of compound interest with a scenario where the initial contribution is $300 and a monthly contribution of $50 is made. Let's also assume the annual interest rate is 12% – which isn't uncommon. Let's also assume that the interest is compounded monthly.

Month 1:
Initial amount: $300
Monthly contribution: $50
Monthly interest (12% / 12): $300 * (0.01) = $3
Total at the end of the month: $300 + $50 + $3 = $353

Month 2:
Initial amount: $353 (previous month's total)
Monthly contribution: $50
Monthly interest: $353 * (0.01) = $3.53
Total at the end of the month: $353 + $50 + $3.53 = $406.53

Month 3:
Initial amount: $406.53 (previous month's total)
Monthly contribution: $50
Monthly interest: $406.53 * (0.01) = $4.07
Total at the end of the month: $406.53 + $50 + $4.07 = $460.60

In just 3 months, you'll have earned an additional $10 on your investment. That's free money and the amount is only going to keep getting larger. In 12 months, you'll have roughly $972.18, giving you an additional $72.18 in returns. Now, that might seem like a small figure, but the more you contribute each month, the more compound interest you get back. If you were to contribute $300 every month, for example, you would get back $242.80 on top of what you've invested ($3,900). The more money you're able to put into your investment each month, the better your return. And you don't have to limit yourself to a fixed payment. In most cases, you can opt for a flexi deposit with a minimum amount to deposit each month. This means that when you have more to contribute, you can really capitalize on compound interest.

Imagine a snowball rolling downhill – picking up speed and size. As mentioned earlier, compound interest works just like that. It multiplies your money over time as you keep reinvesting your earnings. If you're eyeing that beachfront villa at 65, compound interest is your ticket. Start early and your money will work overtime so you can sip coconut water in style.

But, if you want that villa in the near future, the next couple of chapters are going to be more your speed. Nonetheless, start investing now so that you always have that safety net in future no matter what happens on your entrepreneurial journey today. At the end of the day, whether it's a swanky pad, Ivy League education for the kids, or globetrotting adventures, compound interest can make your dreams a reality and it can do it faster than you'd believe.

The major uptick of this is that if you invest a large enough amount and diversify your investments, you can live off the interest. Again, this all comes down to your appetite for risk and whether or not you've hired an astute financial advisor to help you along the way. Either way, just try to imagine money flowing in while you kick back. Compound interest can help you create a stream of passive income, so you can live the good life now – not just when you're retired.

But it's daunting – we know that.

Put too little into a "safe", low-yield investment and you'll see hardly any progress. Put too much into a "risky", high-yield account and you could lose it all. But it only feels like a gamble because you're not financially literate where investing is concerned. Not only that but reading this book will only get you so far. You need to sit down with a financial advisor and allow them to help you plan for your personal goals. While we can offer broad-spectrum advice, the onus is on you to cultivate that hungry mindset and to get out there yourself. You have to step into a proactive, dominant mindset or you're going to get pulled every which way by advice, blogs, and your own fears.

We will give you a few tips on where to potentially invest, but remember, this is not a substitute for sound financial advice. You have to do the due diligence yourself!

With that said, here are a few places where you can park your cash for compounding wins.

- **Stock Market:** It's where financial rockstars are made. Companies like Apple, Amazon, and Google have a habit of delivering mind-blowing compound returns.

- **Bonds:** Bonds are like the chill sidekick in your investment crew. They offer steady returns and are perfect for balancing out your portfolio.

- **Mutual Funds:** These investment powerhouses pool money from everyone to create a diverse portfolio. It's like joining a buffet where you get a taste of everything.

- **Real Estate:** Whether you're into owning properties or Real Estate Investment Trusts (REITs), you can enjoy rental income and property appreciation. It's a double win.

- **Retirement Accounts:** Max out your contributions to 401(k)s or IRAs. They're like turbochargers for your retirement savings, with some sweet tax perks.

The stock market is one of the places that will offer you the craziest returns. You could invest in a newbie that becomes an immediate runaway and it ups your return to 50%. That's amazing, but keep in mind that this isn't commonplace. Also, if you're diving into the stock market, you need the right crew. There are a few whose names have been in the heavyweight ring long enough for us to (kinda) safely assume that they'll keep your money safe.

But we'll say it again: do your due diligence!

Now, let's get into those stock brokers:

- **Charles Schwab:** Known for low-cost trading and a smorgasbord of investment options, it's the go-to for beginners and seasoned investors alike.

- **Fidelity:** With an easy-to-use platform and top-notch research tools, Fidelity is your trusty sidekick. It also offers a range of retirement accounts.

- **TD Ameritrade:** No need to break the bank with this one. With no minimum deposit and a user-friendly interface, it's perfect for newbies and active traders.

- **E*TRADE:** E*TRADE's got your back with a robust trading platform, research tools, and a variety of investment options. It's like having a financial wingman.

- **Interactive Brokers:** If you're a trading maverick looking for advanced tools and low-cost trading, Interactive Brokers has your back.

Whomever you go with, compound interest is your secret weapon; your financial sidekick; your ultimate ace in the hole. By consistently reinvesting your earnings and giving time the stage, you can unleash the power of compound interest to fuel your wealth-building goals. Whether you go all-in on the stock market, cozy up to bonds, explore real estate, or max out your retirement accounts, the aim of the game is to start early. Then, you'll need to stay committed and let compound interest be your financial wizard. With a bit of patience and savvy investment choices, you'll watch your wealth skyrocket. This will undoubtedly secure a brighter financial future for you.

But before that wealth can truly multiply, you need to diversify.

Diversify, Diversify, Diversify: The Investing Mantra

What is "diversification" all about? Well, it's like building a well-balanced plate at an all-you-can-eat buffet. We know very few people who would walk into a buffet and load their plates with only one thing. It doesn't make for an enjoyable experience and you'll probably pay for it later – if you catch our drift. No – what you want is a colorful plate. You want a little bit of everything. More importantly, you want a lot of what's easy to digest, like vegetables (moderate to low-risk investments) and a few cuts of meat (riskier or more long-term investments). That's what diversification is all about. It's the practice of spreading your investments across various asset classes to reduce risk and ensure that you're getting the most out of your investment experience.

So, instead of investing everything in a single asset, you should consider spreading your investments across different types of assets, like stocks, bonds, real estate, and more. This is important because diversification is your shield against the unpredictable nature of financial markets. By spreading your investments, you minimize the impact of a single asset's poor performance on your entire portfolio. But it's not just about risk reduction. It's also about optimizing your returns. Diversification allows you to net potential gains from different asset classes that may perform well at different times. Knowing that your portfolio is well-diversified can provide peace of mind. You won't be losing sleep over every market hiccup.

With that broad understanding of diversification, let's run you your playbook.

Diversification Playbook

Asset Classes:
Start by diversifying across different asset classes. These can include stocks, bonds, real estate, cash, and even alternative investments like commodities or cryptocurrencies.

Geography Matters:
Don't limit your investments to a single geographic region. Consider international stocks and bonds to spread your risk globally.

Industry Sectors:
Within the stock market, diversify across various industry sectors like technology, healthcare, finance, and more. This minimizes the impact of sector-specific risks.

Mutual Funds and ETFs:
Consider investing in mutual funds or exchange-traded funds (ETFs) that provide diversification by holding a basket of assets. They're like the buffet of the investment world.

Rebalancing:
Regularly review and rebalance your portfolio. If one asset class has grown significantly, rebalance by selling some of it and investing in underperforming assets to maintain your desired allocation.

Risk Tolerance
Align your diversification strategy with your risk tolerance and financial goals. A more aggressive strategy might include a higher allocation to stocks, while a conservative one may favor bonds.

Time Horizon:
Your investment horizon matters. Longer-term goals may allow for more risk-taking, while short-term goals require a more conservative approach.

When all is said and done, investment portfolio diversification isn't just a fancy term. It's your recipe for financial stability. By spreading your investments across different assets, sectors, and regions, you're building a resilient financial portfolio that can weather storms and net growth opportunities.

If you're still unsure of how to go about this, have a look at an example of diversified portfolios below.

Stocks and Bonds Mix:
60% Stocks: Invest in a mix of large-cap, mid-cap, and small-cap stocks across different sectors.
30% Bonds: Allocate a portion to government, corporate, and municipal bonds to provide stability.
10% Real Estate Investment Trusts (REITs): Add diversification through real estate investments.

Global Portfolio:
40% U.S. Equities: Diversify within the U.S. stock market.
30% International Equities: Invest in developed and emerging market stocks.
20% Bonds: Diversify bond holdings globally.
10% Commodities: Include precious metals, agricultural products, or energy.

Target-Date Retirement Fund:
Automatically Adjusting Allocations: A target-date fund adjusts its asset allocation over time, becoming more conservative as the investor approaches retirement. It typically includes a mix of stocks and bonds.

Sector-Specific Diversification:
Technology Stocks: Invest in leading technology companies.
Healthcare Stocks: Allocate funds to pharmaceuticals, biotech, and healthcare services.
Consumer Staples: Include companies that produce essential goods.

Dividend-Focused Portfolio:
High Dividend Stocks: Invest in stocks with a history of consistent dividends.
Dividend-Paying ETFs: Include exchange-traded funds that focus on high-dividend stocks.
Dividend Growth Stocks: Allocate to companies with a track record of increasing dividends.

Balanced Portfolio:
50% Equities: Diversify among different stocks.
40% Bonds: Include a mix of government and corporate bonds.
10% Alternatives: Add exposure to hedge funds, private equity, or other alternative investments.

Remember, diversification isn't a one-size-fits-all approach. Tailor it to your risk tolerance, financial goals, and time horizon. And don't forget to review and adjust your diversification strategy as your circumstances change. Never forget what we said earlier – the game is constantly changing and you need to be ready to adapt. This is precisely why we recommend reaching out to a financial advisor. This is a full-time job! You already have one, so don't try to go it alone.

Now that we've brought up the types of stocks and other investments that you should consider, we can delve deeper into them.

From Stocks to Real Estate: Cracking the Investment Code

Now we can turn up the heat a little. From traditional stocks and bonds to the exciting world of property investment and even cryptocurrencies, we're going to explore all the investment avenues available to you – starting with traditional investments. Consider this next section your encyclopedia on core investment terminology and vehicles.

Traditional Investments

Stocks

Stocks represent ownership in a company. When you own shares of a company's stock, you become a shareholder and have the potential to earn money through dividends or by selling your shares at a higher price than you paid. Stocks are known for their potential for high returns but also come with higher risk.

Bonds

Bonds are like IOUs issued by governments or corporations. When you buy a bond, you're lending money to the issuer in exchange for periodic interest payments and the return of the bond's face value when it matures. Bonds are generally considered lower-risk investments than stocks.

Real Estate

Investing in real estate involves purchasing physical properties like homes, apartments, commercial buildings, or land. Real estate can provide rental income and the potential for property appreciation. It's a tangible and often less volatile asset class. You can also use the

BRRR method to buy, refurbish, rent, and refinance property to get a nice chunk of cash out of your investment fairly quickly.

REITs (Real Estate Investment Trusts)

REITs are a way to invest in real estate without owning physical properties. These trusts pool investors' money to buy, manage, and generate income from various real estate assets. REITs typically offer high dividend yields.

Precious Metals

Investing in precious metals like gold and silver can be a hedge against inflation and economic uncertainty. These metals have intrinsic value and can be held physically or through exchange-traded funds (ETFs).

Municipal Bonds

Municipal bonds are debt securities issued by state and local governments. They offer tax advantages and can provide a steady stream of income.

Corporate Bonds

Corporate bonds are issued by companies to raise capital. They offer regular interest payments and the return of the principal amount at maturity.

Alternative Investments

Cryptocurrencies

Cryptocurrencies like Bitcoin and Ethereum have taken the financial world by storm. These digital assets operate on blockchain technology and can be traded on cryptocurrency exchanges. They offer the potential for high returns but come with significant volatility.

Commodities

Commodities include physical goods like oil, gas, agricultural products, and metals. You can invest in commodities directly by purchasing the physical goods or indirectly through commodity ETFs or futures contracts.

Hedge Funds

Hedge funds are pooled investment funds that employ various strategies to generate returns. They often have higher fees and are typically open only to accredited investors due to their complexity and risk.

Private Equity

Private equity involves investing in private companies that are not publicly traded. Private equity firms typically acquire, invest in, and manage these companies with the goal of improving their performance and eventually selling them for a profit.

Which of these are the best investments? Again, that all depends on your goals as well as the level of risk that you're comfortable with. When you start talking about things like risk, it's important that you stick to your guns. This is especially true if you're the type of person to kick themselves when something goes wrong. Make sure that you're only investing money that you don't need. If you're stretching yourself too thin, you're going to suffer from burnout, frustration, or at least some form of mental exhaustion before the year is up. And to make matters worse, some of these investments (like retirement annuities) require monthly upkeep for the foreseeable future.

Take the 401(k), for example. This is a retirement savings plan offered by employers. It allows employees to contribute a portion of their salary on a tax-deferred basis. Employers may also provide matching contributions. An alternative to this is an IRA – or Individual Retirement Account. IRAs are individual retirement savings accounts that offer tax advantages similar to 401(k)s. Traditional IRAs allow tax-deferred contributions, while Roth IRAs provide tax-free withdrawals in retirement. In short, you're saving money from the tax man and enjoying it tax-free later on.

For those of you who have kids, this next one is important. They're called 529 plans and they are tax-advantaged savings accounts designed for education expenses. They can be used for college tuition, books, and other qualified education expenses. Contributions grow tax-free when used for educational purposes. But we're not done yet. There are also countless other investments that are steadily increasing in popularity, so let's tap into them now.

Increasingly Popular Investments

ESG (Environmental, Social, and Governance) Investing
ESG investing involves considering a company's environmental, social, and governance practices when making investment decisions. It aligns with ethical and sustainable values.

Venture Capital
Venture capital firms invest in early-stage companies with high growth potential. They provide funding in exchange for equity ownership.

Angel Investing
Angel investors are individuals who provide capital to startups in exchange for ownership equity. They often play a crucial role in helping startups grow.

Art, Collectibles, and Antiques

Investing in art, rare collectibles, or antiques can be a passion-driven investment. These assets can appreciate in value over time, but their market can be less liquid.

Peer-to-Peer (P2P) Lending

P2P lending platforms connect borrowers with individual lenders. Investors can earn interest by funding loans to individuals or small businesses.

Foreign Exchange (Forex)

Forex trading involves the buying and selling of currencies in the foreign exchange market. It's highly speculative and requires a good understanding of currency markets.

To sum up, as you navigate the investment landscape, remember that diversification is your ally. A well-diversified portfolio can help manage risk and optimize returns. Also, consider your financial goals, risk tolerance, and investment horizon when choosing the right mix of investments for your portfolio. Each investment option has its unique characteristics, benefits, and risks. It's crucial to do your due diligence and, if necessary, seek advice from financial professionals to make informed investment decisions that align with your financial objectives.

So, what are you waiting for? Go out there and make some financial magic happen!

While you're at it, look into making your entrepreneurial dreams happen with OPM in the next chapter.

Chapter 6 – OPM: Other People's Money – The Entrepreneur's Secret Weapon

---

Let's talk OPM. This is your secret weapon to building the life of your dreams. And we know what you're already thinking – this sounds nefarious and insidious. This is because we have such an unhealthy relationship with money. People all over the world – irrespective of creed, religion, or social standing – consider money to be a bit of a touchy subject. We don't talk about how much we earn because we don't want to brag. We don't ask others how much they earn because we don't want to be nosey. We definitely don't expect anyone to give us money to better our lives because that would be greedy.

While most of this has merit and we get the sentiments behind it all, we've all been fed a lie.

You see, the thing is, wealthy people have been borrowing money to make themselves wealthier since the dawn of currency. It's just how this game is played. How so? Well, let's look at a simple example. Let's say you own a business that makes $300,000 in profit for the year. Instead of paying tax on that amount, you could purchase a property in your business's name. This then becomes an asset to your business. Then, you could go to the bank and mortgage $300,000 against your business asset (the property).

Why would you do that?

You already had that amount of money. Why would you take out a loan and incur all of that interest?

Because loans are tax-free money. If you play your cards right (and have a tenant in that property to pay off the mortgage and interest for you) you'll never lose a dime of that initial $300,000 profit. If you're currently paying rent for your business, you could use this as your business premises and your business could pay itself back as opposed to paying someone else rent.

Of course, there are only so many times you can do this, but it's all about getting creative and removing the ceilings from above your potential. Now that we have your attention, let's dig deeper into the premise of borrowing to build.

Borrowing to Build: The Mindset Shift You Need

This is the dynamic strategy that can turbocharge your wealth-building journey in nothing flat. It's called borrowing money to invest and it's a powerful technique but, like any adventure, it comes with its challenges and risks. But before any of those risks and rewards can come to fruition, you need to get on the level with tax efficiency. Tax laws and strategies can be complex, but understanding them can save you a significant amount of money. Not knowing the means of tax-efficient investing and financial planning can result in higher tax bills and this will reduce your overall wealth.

We'll state this again – we're not legal professionals nor are we financial advisors. While this book is chock full of tips and tricks to get you thinking like a financial shark, you still need to carve out your own path. Think of it this way – there are millions of books in the world and thousands of different concepts on how to grow your wealth. One book couldn't simply change your life without you putting in the effort and aligning yourself with the path that suits you. We're just here to detail all of the means in brief. You have to go deeper. As such, we recommend sitting down with an estate planner or a tax attorney (or both) to figure out the best way to safeguard your investments.

When you've done this, you can tap into the power of leverage for financial gain. Leverage is the strategy of using borrowed money to amplify your investment returns. And when we say investment, we mean anything you put your money into in order to see a return – that could be stocks, bonds, or even business ventures of your own.

Leverage can truly supercharge your gains. If your investment performs well, you'll earn returns not only on your own money but also on the borrowed funds. Be warned, though. If you borrow money with high interest tied to it, you might only make enough of a return to cover the total loan amount inclusive of that interest. In worst-case scenarios, you might only be able to cover the initial loan amount and not the interest – and we all know what happens when interest compounds.

That said, if you have access to a low-interest – or no-interest – loan, then this can help you scale up your investments faster. With leverage, you can enter bigger markets and seize opportunities that might have been out of reach otherwise. Always remember that what you borrow will need to be paid back whether or not the investment pays off. So, borrow what you can afford to pay back in a worst-case scenario and try to stick to investments that have a high probability of success.

If, on the other hand, you're not necessarily looking for a "big fish" but you're just hoping to spread out your investments across different asset classes, this is also a great option. Just remember that borrowed money isn't free money. You're on the hook for repayment and if your investments tank, you might find yourself drowning in debt. Borrowing to invest in high-risk ventures is a recipe for financial disaster. Even if the reward seems like the best thing this side of sliced bread, always know that if something looks too good to be true, it usually is.

Moreover, you need to be aware of how your credit score impacts your ability to borrow. Have a look at the credit score-to-interest ratios below.

720-850	10.7% - 12.5%
690-719	13.5% - 15.5%
630-689	17.8% - 19.9%
300-629	28.5% - 32%

Table 3: Credit Score to Interest Rate Ratios

So, the lower your credit score, the more interest your lender will tack onto your loan. This is why it's crucial to correct your credit score and clean up your credit report before attempting to borrow any more money or ask for any further lines of credit. But there is another borrowing avenue to get you going. It involves property investment as your first step.

Let's look into it.

Low-Interest Lending Scenario

Find a property in a modest neighborhood for about $280,000. It could be anything – an apartment, condo, or single-room unit. Depending on the bank that you're able to get a mortgage with as well as your credit score, you could potentially bag an interest rate in the region of 5%-7.8%. (If you ask us, that's a lot better than 32%!)

Once you've bought the unit, get a tenant in there as fast as possible. Allow them to pay the mortgage down and send additional payments of your own to your bank to bring this down further. In a couple of years (when you have more equity in the property), refinance your property to its current value. You can then use that money to invest in other areas while your tenant remains in place and pays that off for you once again.

It's important to note that this only works if you've locked in a fixed interest rate on that mortgage. If you do, you can use that property as your personal piggy bank for the rest of your life. As time goes on, the property will continuously appreciate in value. This – along with the regular payments – will increase your equity in the property over time. If you never make that final payment and, instead, take your equity out of the property every time you're about to pay the property off, you'll have money to reinvest...forever. And this is all while someone else (your tenant) foots the bill. As mentioned in the opening section of this chapter, you have to get creative with financing your dreams – and property investment is a relatively low-risk way to do this.

So let's recap the rules of engagement in your money-borrowing blueprint.

- **Guaranteed Returns:** Only consider borrowing if the returns are almost guaranteed. It might sound like a paradox, but in the world of investments, nothing is ever truly guaranteed. So, opt for investments with a strong track record and stable returns.

- **Diversify Your Portfolio:** Don't put all your borrowed eggs in one investment basket. Diversify across different assets to spread risk. This way, a loss in one area can be offset by gains in another.

- **Risk Assessment:** Be brutally honest about your risk tolerance. High-risk, high-reward investments may sound enticing, but they can also lead to significant losses when leveraged. Make sure you can sleep at night with your investment choices.

- **Affordability Check:** Borrow only what you can comfortably afford to pay back, even if your investments don't perform as expected. Remember, you're still responsible for repaying the borrowed funds.

- **Interest Rates Matter:** Pay close attention to the interest rates on your borrowed funds. High-interest loans can quickly erode your returns, making leverage less effective.

Just remember to maintain a robust emergency fund to cover unexpected expenses and loan repayments. This way, you won't be forced to sell off your investments in a downturn. The bottom line is that borrowing money to build wealth can be a game-changing strategy, but it's not for the faint of heart. It requires a deep understanding of your risk tolerance, meticulous planning, and a disciplined approach to repayments. Plus, leverage isn't a one-size-fits-all solution. It's a tool in your financial toolbox and its effectiveness depends on how you use it.

Navigating Business Credit, Loans, and Angel Investors

Everything we've mentioned up until now will require some type of business structure in order to take shape. While there a various types of business structures that you could benefit from, if you'll be going this route alone, we would suggest setting up an LLC. This is because an LLC offers you protection from debt. If your business goes bust, for example, the assets that you've registered in your personal capacity (in your name) are safe. Be sure to look into what business entity would suit you best and your financial needs best, then you can set to work on cultivating your business credit.

Your business's creditworthiness is like its financial resume. Building a strong business credit profile can open doors to various funding opportunities. But you have to play by the rules – the first of which is to keep your personal and business finances separate. Obtain a federal Employer Identification Number (EIN) and open a business bank account. Then, be sure to float all of your business expenses via your business bank account and keep records of your expenditure as well as your income. This will help you submit your tax returns with a substantial number of items that you can write off from your tax bill.

For those of you who aren't already aware, business tax write-offs (also known as deductions) are expenses that a business incurs during its operations. In other words, it's everything that you spend to keep your business going and this can be subtracted from the business's total income to determine its taxable income. The lower the taxable income, the less the business has to pay in taxes. We'll give you a few examples of tax-deductible expenses.

Operating Expenses:

What it is: Everyday costs of running your business.

Examples: Rent, utilities, office supplies, employee salaries, insurance, and advertising.

How it works: These expenses directly relate to the day-to-day operations of the business and can be deducted from the total income.

Cost of Goods Sold (COGS):

What it is: Costs directly associated with producing goods or services.

Examples: Raw materials, labor directly involved in production, and manufacturing overhead.

How it works: For businesses that sell products, the cost of producing those products can be deducted.

Business Vehicle Expenses:

What it is: Costs related to using vehicles for business purposes.

Examples: Gas, maintenance, and depreciation of business vehicles.

How it works: If you use a vehicle for business, you can deduct the costs associated with its use.

Home Office Expenses:

What it is: Expenses related to a portion of your home used exclusively for business.

Examples: Mortgage interest, property taxes, utilities, and maintenance for the business portion of your home.

How it works: If you use part of your home exclusively for your business, you may be able to deduct related expenses.

Meals and Entertainment:

What it is: Costs associated with meals and entertainment for business purposes.

Examples: Business meals, client entertainment.

How it works: Typically, only a percentage of these expenses is deductible.

Depreciation:

What it is: The gradual decrease in the value of assets over time.

Examples: Depreciation of business equipment, machinery, or vehicles.

How it works: Businesses can deduct a portion of the cost of certain assets over their useful life.

Business Travel Expenses:

What it is: Costs associated with business-related travel.

Examples: Airfare, hotel accommodations, meals while traveling for business.

How it works: Travel expenses incurred for business purposes are generally deductible.

Interest on Business Loans:

What it is: Interest paid on loans taken for business purposes.

Examples: Interest on business loans or credit cards used for business expenses.

How it works: The interest paid on loans used for business purposes is typically deductible.

Knowing your tax-deductible expenses will help you save money in the long run. From there, you can consider leveraging business credit to help keep your business running. What business – you might ask?

Whatever you can set your mind to!

Even running those property investments themselves can be a business. It all boils down to your ability to start thinking outside the box and getting creative with your funds. Consider using business credit cards to establish a credit history for your company. Make payments on time and keep credit utilization low. Establish relationships with vendors and suppliers who report payment history to business credit bureaus. Finally, just as you've done with your personal credit, regularly check your business credit reports and dispute any inaccuracies. This ensures your credit profile accurately reflects your financial responsibility.

Now, for larger business pursuits, you're going to want to consider business loans. When it comes to these loans, there's a plethora of options tailored to different needs. We'll explore some of the more common ones below.

Term Loans	These provide a lump sum upfront, which you repay over a fixed term with interest.
Lines of Credit	Like a credit card for your business, you can borrow up to a predetermined limit and only pay interest on the amount used.
SBA Loans	Backed by the U.S. Small Business Administration, these loans offer favorable terms and lower interest rates.
Microloans	Small loans provided by nonprofit organizations or micro-lending institutions, often for startups and small businesses.
Equipment Financing	Loans specifically for purchasing equipment or machinery.

Table 4: Types of Business Loans

These are great for scaling your business – especially if you run a traditional business. However, e-commerce businesses are recognized as official businesses in the US. So, don't go thinking that you need a brick-and-mortar business to get funding because you don't. However, if you find difficulty acquiring a loan and you need it before your business credit history has had the time to accumulate, you can turn to angel investors. These are high-net-worth individuals who provide capital to startups in exchange for equity ownership.

To bring these financial angels on board, you'll need to put together a compelling business pitch that highlights your vision, market potential, and how their investment can make a difference. Wealthy people don't stay wealthy by handing out huge sums of cash to anyone who asks them for it. More importantly, they've been through the financial wringer themselves, so they can spot a weak proposal a mile away. In fact, they may have written some of their own back when they were trying to come up, so actually do your homework. Better yet, get someone to help you with the research elements if that's not your strong point.

With a pitch in mind and on hand, start attending industry events and join entrepreneurship groups to expand your network and connect with potential angel investors. But don't just walk around these events handing your card or business pitch out to people. Those days are long gone. Now, you have to build relationships first. Yes, this is going to take time, but it will also show you who (in these circles) actually has the potential to invest in you and who's just all talk.

If you're having a hard time finding these circles in the first place, you might want to find a mentor first. Word to the wise, don't pay someone to mentor you. If you have to pay them to mentor you, chances are that they're not actually who they say they are. And we're not talking about life coaches here because that's a whole different story, which we'll discuss in Chapter 10.

Instead, try to find a mentor on platforms like LinkedIn. You can also go the old-fashioned route of just being at the right place at the right time. Sign up for a gym membership in an affluent part of town. Go to a coffee shop in the financial district during your lunch hour. "Bump into" the crowd that you're looking for and gradually strike up a conversation.

When you have someone who's interested in investing in you, remember that angel investors conduct thorough due diligence. Be prepared to share financial data, projections, and a solid business plan. Negotiate terms that align with your business's growth goals while ensuring a fair deal for both of you. But don't be so desperate to do something that you take on exorbitantly high-interest loans. This isn't your only option, so if people simply aren't playing with you, try our next funding option: crowdfunding.

In recent years, crowdfunding has emerged as a popular way to raise capital. It involves pitching your business idea to a crowd of online investors, which can include friends and family. There are different crowdfunding models, including rewards-based (offering perks to backers), equity crowdfunding (selling shares), and donation-based (asking for financial support without offering returns). You'll need to choose a crowdfunding platform that aligns with your business model. Popular platforms include Kickstarter, Indiegogo, and SeedInvest. Just like the business plan that you've poured your time into, you'll need to craft an engaging crowdfunding campaign with a captivating video, clear rewards, and a compelling story. As for promoting your campaign, social media, email newsletters, and outreach to potential backers is the way to go. Keep your backers up to date so that they feel like they are more than just financially invested in you. If all else fails, you can set your sights on grants – non-repayable funds provided to businesses for specific purposes.

If this piques your interest, here's what you need to know. Grants aren't just given to anyone who wants to start up a business. Your business will likely have to innovate in a certain underperforming sector or solve a real-world problem. The U.S. government offers various grant programs for businesses, particularly those engaged in research, innovation, or social impact. If you plan on operating a business in any of these areas, you can try to find and apply for one of the following:

1. **State and Local Grants:** Many states and localities have grant programs to support businesses, often focusing on job creation and economic development.

2. **Private Grants:** Private foundations and organizations also offer grants, often with specific missions or goals in mind.

But applying for grants can be competitive. Ensure that you meet all of the eligibility criteria and follow application guidelines diligently. It's equally important for you to do your own digging when it comes to grants because this landscape changes on the daily. A grant that was available at the time of publishing this book might not be available by the time you read this book. You can set up Google Alerts for grants in your area of interest and that will free up the time it will take you to do your own research on a near-daily basis.

Ultimately, navigating the world of business credit, loans, angel investors, crowdfunding, and grants can be a multifaceted journey. Each option offers unique advantages and considerations. As you chart your course, consider your business's financial needs, growth objectives, and risk tolerance. Remember that building a strong business credit profile is just like building a strong personal credit profile in that it's an ongoing process. Choose loans that align with your funding requirements and repayment capacity. That is how you'll successfully launch and scale your business. Speaking of scaling, let's dive into the principles of scaling up using OPM in greater detail now.

Scaling Up: The Art of Using OPM to Your Advantage

As you already know, OPM refers to the practice of using external funds, such as loans, investments, or borrowed capital, to expand and scale your business. It's a strategic approach that can send your business soaring to new heights. But it is an art and one that you need to master.

First off, you need to understand that what we said earlier holds true. Wealthy people don't stay wealthy by handing their money out to any-old-body who comes asking them for it. They want to know that they can trust you but they also want to see that you've done your homework. Even when those two boxes are ticked, they might want to have their hand in guiding the business safely out of the dock and through what are likely uncharted waters for you.

In most cases, this is a good thing.

Investors and lenders often bring valuable expertise and connections to the table. This can enhance your business's chances of success. It's all too easy to get cocky in the beginning and to think that no one knows your business better than you do, but if you're trying to be the only smart person in the room, you're doing it all wrong. You should want to know more about how things work instead of trying to pull the reins all on your own.

Do you honestly think your business idea is so good that this person is going to steal it right out from under you if you don't show them who's "boss"? No. They've got better things to do and you're the one who approached them, remember. Yes, always put everything in writing and safeguard your intellectual property because...you never know. However, also allow yourself to be teachable. If you can't bootstrap your own business, you'll need to learn a thing or two about humility.

With that out of the way, here are the types of OPM you can get your hands on:

- **Equity Financing:** Equity financing involves selling shares or ownership stakes in your business to investors in exchange for capital. Common sources of equity financing include angel investors, venture capitalists, and crowdfunding.

- **Debt Financing:** Debt financing involves borrowing money that you'll repay with interest. Traditional lenders, such as banks, offer business loans, while alternative lenders and peer-to-peer platforms provide additional options.

- **Strategic Partnerships:** Partnering with other businesses or individuals can bring financial resources and synergies that enhance your business's growth. These partnerships may involve joint ventures, licensing agreements, or co-marketing efforts.

But before seeking OPM, have a clear vision for your business. Define your goals, target market, and growth strategy. Investors and lenders want to see a well-thought-out plan. Also, understand your financials inside and out. Know your business's valuation, cash flow projections, and how you plan to use the funds you're seeking.

Put it all on paper – especially your repayment strategy. In this regard, nothing could be more important than having a well-defined plan for repaying the borrowed capital, including interest. If equity is involved, consider your long-term strategy. How will you provide returns to equity investors or repay lenders? Having a clear exit plan demonstrates your commitment to honoring financial agreements. This is why it's vital that you sit down with an expert whenever you're taking on something like this. Consult with legal professionals to create agreements that protect your interests and clarify expectations.

Finally, before we wrap up this chapter, let's look at some popular OPM success stories.

Airbnb

Airbnb used angel investments and venture capital funding to scale from a small startup to a global hospitality giant, raising billions in OPM along the way.

Facebook

Facebook secured early investments from venture capitalists, which fueled its growth from a college networking platform to a social media behemoth.

Chapter 6

To sum up, using other people's money to scale your business is a strategic art that can elevate your entrepreneurial journey. Whether through equity financing, debt financing, partnerships, or a combination of these methods, OPM can provide the fuel needed to propel your business to new heights. Just be cautious. Approach all of this with careful planning, clear goals, and risk mitigation strategies in place. And don't forget to build strong relationships with your investors and lenders – and always maintain transparency in your financial dealings!

Once you start growing in the financial sense, it'll be time to break the rules.

CHAPTER 7 – RULE BREAKER: ALWAYS DEVELOP MULTIPLE STREAMS OF INCOME

Now you're getting it! You're starting to see that there isn't anything special about the people who go on to become incredibly wealthy other than their knowledge of how the money system works. For many of the people who have gone on to become millionaires (and billionaires) all they needed was to just get their foot in the door. When you have money, it's easy to make more. When you know how to use other people's money, this becomes way easier to achieve.

But there's a reason why you might have thought that billionaires had some special skill that put them head and shoulders above the rest. The media.

The media is so good at painting this picture of perfection and telling you that these people are star athletes, prolific talk show hosts, and incredible inventors. Athletes without this knowledge will look at other athletes and wonder what their secret is. They'll say, "What am I doing wrong?" You might look at your colleagues or age mates who are able to travel the world and think "We earn in a similar bracket – why can't I afford to do that?"

First off, don't compare yourself to others. Envy is the road to anger and despair. Moreover, you don't have the full picture. These people aren't just living off their primary earnings. Instead, the majority of them have multiple streams of income that they use to supplement their lifestyles. Just take a look at Jeff Bezos. Yes, Amazon has really boomed in the last decade, but Amazon still makes losses (not profits) year on year. In 2022 alone, they reported a net loss of $2.7 billion [7]. That doesn't mean Bezos is going to be selling his mansions or his stake in the company anytime soon. He has other streams of income that supplement his lifestyle. That way, he can focus on keeping Amazon afloat without making drastic decisions due to personal financial desperation.

This is a strategy that you need to adopt to keep yourself growing from financial strength to strength. But despite the fact that you're beginning to see how the system is run, you're not quite there yet. There is still some legwork to do before you become a true money master who can hustle their way to financial freedom.

So, let's delve into the inner workings of income diversification.

The Safety Net: Why Diversification Is Non-Negotiable

Just as you'll diversify your investments, you also need to diversify your income streams. In this day and age, it's simply non-negotiable. What our parents experienced and what we're now living through is chalk and cheese. Back then, a teacher and a firefighter could buy a 3-bedroom home in the burbs with a big ol' backyard and treehouse for good measure. Now, high-powered professionals are struggling to purchase that same property. Things just aren't the same anymore.

So, if you think you're going to rely on one income for the rest of your life, think again. Even if things are comfortable for you right now, ask yourself how close you are to the knife's edge. If one of your major expenses goes up by just 10%, how comfortable are you going to be?

Yes, for generations, the traditional 9-to-5 job was seen as the pinnacle of financial security and comfort. However, job security is no longer a guarantee.

Now, having multiple income sources provides financial freedom and flexibility. You're not solely dependent on a single employer or client, which means you have more control over your financial destiny. These different income streams can offer diverse opportunities. Some may provide stable, consistent income, while others may offer the potential for rapid growth or passive earnings.

The great thing is that on top of upping your earnings, pursuing various income streams often requires acquiring new skills and expanding your knowledge base. This continuous learning can enhance your personal and professional development, which is of the utmost importance if you want to continue evolving and staying ahead of potential recessions.

But don't just take our word for it. Have a look around at what everyone else is doing. A recent survey showed that a whopping 39% of all Americans who are formally (and informally) employed now have **at least** one side hustle [11]. Things are tough out there right now and we get it. We're not some random rich guy telling you to stop buying coffee and how that will make all of your financial problems go away. Nor are we touting that the current economic climate is in any way your fault – because it isn't. However, we are saying that you need to take things into your own hands and we're giving you real-world advice that applies to changing your financial trajectory with the cards you have right now – not some old-school cards where you could buy a house for the price of a Grande Macchiato.

We're being facetious, but you get it.

Let's move on to some of the more common sources of multiple income streams.

- **Primary Job:** Your primary job, whether as an employee or self-employed, is often your main income source.

- **Side Hustles:** Side gigs, freelance work, or part-time jobs can supplement your primary income.

- **Investments:** Income from investments, such as dividends, interest, or rental income, can provide ongoing cash flow.

- **Business Ventures:** If you run a business, income from various products, services, or revenue streams within the business contributes to your overall earnings.

- **Passive Income:** Passive income, like royalties from intellectual property, affiliate marketing, or real estate investments, can generate money without active daily involvement.

- **Online Earnings:** Income from online ventures, such as blogging, content creation, e-commerce, or affiliate marketing, can be highly scalable.

We've touched on all of these, right?

No? So, which one haven't we discussed?

That's correct – online earnings. While we've hinted at e-commerce and the potential to earn online, we haven't explored this just yet. We are going to get into this in the next chapter, so let's keep it going with why income diversification is important.

For one thing, the risk of overreliance on a single income source can be substantial. If your primary income source tanks, you may find yourself in a precarious financial situation with limited options. Add to this the fact that relying solely on one income stream can lead to financial stagnation and you've got disaster on the cards. There's limited room for growth or innovation when you're tied to a single source. This means that by focusing solely on one source of income, you may miss out on other lucrative opportunities that could diversify your earnings.

Trust us, there is a method to the madness and it starts with a self-evaluation. Assess your skills and talents to identify potential income-generating opportunities. From there, you can define your financial goals and create a plan for achieving them through various income streams. It's always wise to begin with manageable side hustles or investments. As you gain experience and confidence, you can explore more diverse opportunities. The important thing is that you do not stop learning along the way. Don't start to think that you're in any way superior to anybody else or get a big head over what you've learned and accomplished. Remember that you were once where others find themselves right now and that you had to learn by doing. Seeing things this way will keep you humble and will encourage you to invest in your education and skill development. Always remember that acquiring new knowledge can open doors to additional income sources.

With this belief firmly in your mind, you can continue building a strong professional network to discover new income opportunities and collaborations. Just try to effectively manage your time to balance multiple income streams without burnout. If you want our advice on the matter, focus more on setting up passive income streams first. Then, you can dive into more demanding income streams when you have more time and clarity of mind.

Overall, by diversifying your income portfolio, you can take control of your financial future, reduce risk, and open doors to a wealth of possibilities. We can learn from the 2020 pandemic about what not to do – and one of the things that we should no longer be doing is relying on a sole source of income.

Learning from the Pandemic: What Not to Do

The world is in a state of constant evolution. Technology, industries, and job markets are rapidly changing. In this landscape, the ability to learn and adapt is no longer a luxury but a necessity for financial security. As we said, if there is one thing that the pandemic taught us it's that these companies will throw you overboard in the blink of an eye in a bid to save themselves. They're not going to go down with the ship over you and your financial security. They will cut people indiscriminately because human resources are often the largest chunk out of their pockets each month and the quickest one to cut in an economic downturn.

If you're currently employed and you feel like you wouldn't have anywhere else to go if you lost your job, this is a sign that you need to start acquiring some new skills. Upskilling is a potent tool for income diversification. This is because learning new skills keeps you relevant in your current job or industry. It makes you a valuable asset to employers. Even if you run your own business or you're a one-man band, upskilling makes you an invaluable resource to your clients. The more knowledgeable you are, the more readily you can answer their industry-related questions. This is a big one because it doesn't just take great customer service to keep your clients. It also takes trust and they will trust you more if you seem like a safe haven for their questions.

Other than that, acquiring skills outside of your primary field can unlock new income opportunities. For example, a marketer could learn web development to expand into digital marketing. When you can become more of a one-stop shop for employers and clients alike, you are more likely to be a little more indispensable than the person who doesn't make the same effort. Plus, new skills can lead to side hustles or freelance work in areas where you have expertise – and we all know how important side hustles can be nowadays.

Speaking of which, the gig economy thrives on diverse skills. It's a playground for income diversification, offering various platforms and opportunities for those willing to learn. Platforms like Upwork and Fiverr offer income streams for writers, designers, programmers, and more. If you have a knack for teaching, you can become an online tutor or instructor. The good news is that you don't necessarily have to be in a teaching field in order to do this and you'll see just what we mean by this in Chapters 9 and 10. Essentially, certain fields only require simple certifications (which are quick to acquire) and you'll be on your way.

The point is that you need to get fierce about your life. Get angry when people tell you that you need them and get busy making sure that you never need them again. Yes, reach out to people who care about you for help, and don't be afraid to follow a mentor or coach's guidance, but don't you ever let anyone hold power over your life and financial well-being. You are just as powerful as the next person and you can learn new skills no matter how old you are or what your background is.

Always be aware that education, whether formal or informal, is an investment in yourself and your income potential. But on the flip side of that coin, also know that you do not need an Ivy League education to become wealthy, so don't go broke on a degree that may or may not pay off in the long run. Use the resources at your disposal and don't go into debt in the belief that it will help you make more money. And don't think a degree will safeguard you from getting laid off either. That's like jumping into a pool and thinking you won't get wet just because you jumped in with an umbrella.

With that said, there are affordable means of upskilling and they include the following:

- **Online Courses:** Platforms like Coursera, edX, and Udemy offer a vast array of courses on diverse subjects.

- **Certifications:** Earning certifications in fields like project management, digital marketing, or data analysis can increase your earning potential.

Keep yourself moving and stay on your toes. That doesn't mean you should walk around feeling anxious about the future, but try to put measures in place that ensure you'll never have to worry. Consider it your income insurance. Anything can change in a flash and you don't want to get caught with your pants down in the process. After all, the COVID-19 pandemic accelerated the need for remote work and online skills. Millions of people discovered that they could learn and work from anywhere. Moreover, they needed remote skills to see them through the proverbial storm. Skills like remote team management, virtual collaboration, and online project management became essential. What's more, companies that thrived during the pandemic often had employees who embraced digital transformation and learned new digital tools.

But the crux of the matter comes down to the joy of lifelong learning. Continuous learning isn't just about income diversification. It's a source of personal growth and satisfaction. You can cultivate curiosity in order to keep your mind engaged and open to new ideas or you can tell yourself that learning is a chore that you have no interest in. Whatever you choose, just know this: lifelong learners are more adaptable to change – both in their careers and personal lives. Learning new skills also builds resilience, thus, allowing you to bounce back from setbacks.

The 2020 pandemic served as a stark reminder that life is unpredictable. Jobs were lost, businesses shuttered, and economic stability crumbled for many. It was a wake-up call that highlighted the dangers of relying on a single income source. Those solely dependent on traditional employment were left in financial turmoil when layoffs and furloughs occurred. Without supplementary income sources, financial stress and uncertainty mounted in a matter of weeks – not months or years…**WEEKS**.

In the end, this was a wake-up call for everyone who lived through it. The world was changed forever. Long story short, we're never going back to the pre-pandemic days and we just have to keep moving forward. It's the natural order of things. One thing is for certain, online businesses and side hustles are on the rise and those who embrace this will be safe from the pitfalls of an unstable job market. Don't wait for anyone to give you the green light. Instead, learn to adapt through multiple income streams to take care of you and yours by any means necessary.

Adaptation through Multiple Income Streams - By Any Means Necessary

Time is a precious commodity and how we allocate it reveals a lot about our priorities. Many of us spend the majority of our waking hours working for someone else's dreams – leaving little time for our own. Now, we're not going to say that you have the same 24 hours in the day because someone who has to work long hours and take care of their kids when they get home does not have the same 24 hours in the day as someone who works from home or has a nanny. A new graduate who is trying to climb the corporate ladder and prove themselves does not have the same 24 hours in the day as someone who is established and works in a healthy work environment. All of us have different commitments and for us to tell you what to do with yours would be presumptuous and ludicrous.

We will say this, though: try to find hours in the day when you're not necessarily being productive. No, you do not need to be productive every waking minute of the day. We are all worthy and deserving of rest. However, in the early days – when you're trying to establish multiple income streams, you're going to have to find time just like you're going to have to find the pennies to make things happen.

So, let's talk about digital distractions. In today's 24/7 digital world, it's easy to get lost in a sea of distractions. Hours spent scrolling through social media or binge-watching TV shows can add up quickly. If you have an iPhone, all you need to do is navigate to settings and just have a look at how many hours you spend on your phone every day. If you committed to not using your phone for anything other than emergencies for a week, how many hours would you have to yourself?

We're not asking you to become a hermit, but we encourage you to take control of your time and it begins with a mindful approach to how you use it. Always remember the principle of compounding interest. A little bit of progress each day can add up to big gains in 12 months. Your goals and dreams deserve attention. They represent your aspirations and the life you want to create. Neglecting them can lead to feelings of unfulfillment and regret. Don't do this to yourself.

The truth is that when we're not pouring into our own cups, even the smallest requests can seem astronomical. After an entire day of pouring into yourself – of your coffee going cold 10 times, your train of thought being interrupted 20 times, and missed opportunities – someone asking you to pass them the salt can feel like they're asking you to donate a kidney to them. In other words, it can feel like they're asking for too much. So, if you want your relationships to flourish, your mental health to grow, and your overall sense of self to take a positive turn, you need to prioritize your goals and dreams.

If that involves entrepreneurship, kudos to you! Entrepreneurship often starts with a spark of inspiration. By dedicating time to your passions and interests, you can discover entrepreneurial opportunities you might otherwise miss. However, this also applies to those of you who want to capitalize on passive income streams while maintaining your 9-5. Either way, you need to adopt a "By Any Means Necessary" mindset. The phrase was famously used by civil rights leader and pioneer, Malcolm X, to emphasize the importance of achieving social justice goals no matter the obstacles. We can adapt this mindset to personal growth and entrepreneurship in the following ways:

- **Resourcefulness:** Be resourceful and proactive in your quest for self-improvement. If you lack formal education in a particular field, seek online courses or tutorials.

- **Time Management:** Reevaluate your time management. If you can find hours for leisure, you can certainly allocate some for your goals. Use your smartphone for research, idea generation, or skill development.

- **Self-Care:** Prioritize self-care, including physical and mental well-being. A healthy mind and body are essential for pursuing your goals relentlessly.

There is something that you should know. Resistance to change or fear of the unknown will attempt to hold you back. Human beings don't like to venture into the unknown because it is a safety risk and anything seen as a safety risk is a risk to our survival. Here's a newsflash: we, like any other living organism on earth, are pre-programmed for survival. So, don't let your survival instincts trick you out of doing something that could work in your best interests just because you feel the natural self-preservation mechanism known as resistance to change.

Blow through those initial feelings of discomfort and start small. You can begin by dedicating just a few hours a week to your personal growth and entrepreneurial pursuits. Then, share your goals with a trusted friend or mentor who can hold you accountable. This added support can help you stay on track. And don't forget to visualize the benefits of working on your goals.

What does achieving your dreams look like?

How will it transform your life?

Answer those questions earnestly and don't let anyone guilt trip you out of wanting more out of life. You are worthy of all of the abundance in the world – and then some. We all are. Just keep working on yourself and your goals as diligently (and honestly) as you can and it will all pay off in the end. If supposedly successful people quit when the going got tough, we wouldn't have things like e-commerce, social networks, music, movies, art, or books. Just take J.K. Rowling as an example. Before becoming a literary sensation with the Harry Potter series, she was depressed, living on welfare with her two kids, and suicidal. Not only that but her manuscript for Harry Potter was rejected 12 times!

Our point. You can achieve anything you set your mind to if you just keep trying. The world has a funny way of rewarding the indomitable spirit and championing the underdog. Whether you're living comfortably or struggling to make ends meet doesn't matter. What matters is that you reignite your spark and look for multiple income streams to keep you comfortable for all the days of your life. Never forget that time is your most precious asset, and how you choose to spend it defines your journey.

CHAPTER 8 – E-COMMERCE EMPIRE: CONQUER THE ONLINE MARKETPLACE

We're making progress so let's keep the pace up. At this point, you're going to learn about the ins and outs of e-commerce. Now, in recent years, people have touted that e-commerce is dead. It's an old horse that people keep trying to ride that just ain't going anywhere. They claim that the market is saturated and that there simply is no more room for anyone who wants to break into it.

We'll let you in on a little secret: they're the cynics.

Many of them have a pessimistic outlook on e-commerce because they tried it and failed – most likely because they threw money at the thing without doing any of their *SAY IT WITH US* **due diligence**. Moreover, many people who have tried e-commerce and failed have done so out of sheer desperation. They haven't stuck with it through the learning curves and the potential early losses because they were after quick money.

If you want quick money, you can get (or stick to) a day job.

If you want money that will change your life, you'll need to put in the effort to maintain your current income streams while trying to optimize another. In other words, keep your day job, roll up your sleeves, and get to work on your e-commerce business.

If you, like the cynics and the skeptics, feel like there is no room for you in the e-commerce industry, try this on for size. During the 2020 pandemic, online sales went from 50% of all internet users to 60% [8]. That's a 10% jump in a space of a couple of months. Amazon's sales increased by a whopping 37% [9]. Now, Amazon turns over $1.29 billion in revenue per day. That's $15,000 **PER SECOND** [10].

So, tell us again how e-commerce is dead. We'll wait.

For those of you who know better, let's look at how embracing the 24/7 money-making machine that is e-commerce will change your life.

Embracing E-commerce: 24/7 Money-Making Machine

Let's unpack the basics first. E-commerce, or electronic commerce, is the buying and selling of goods and services over the internet. It's a vast virtual marketplace that transcends geographical limitations, offering a myriad of opportunities for entrepreneurs and consumers alike. Since we offered Amazon as an example, let's keep with it. Amazon was founded by Jeff Bezos in 1994 and it marked the genesis of the e-commerce revolution. Its audacious goal was to be "Earth's most customer-centric company," and it set the stage for a new era of online shopping. But in those early days, Amazon's primary goal was to sell books and CDs.

For those of you who don't know what those are, they're compact discs that store music. Yes, that's how you got your music back then, but since you're reading a financial book, we'll assume that most of you are probably old enough to remember it. Long story short, Amazon introduced the concept of shopping from the comfort of your home with an ever-expanding selection of products and the convenience of doorstep delivery. This seismic shift in consumer behavior paved the way for countless e-commerce ventures.

Then came smartphones and ultra-fast internet. This sent e-commerce into overdrive. With smartphones, consumers can shop on the go – anytime; anywhere. It's like carrying a shopping mall in your pocket. High-speed internet allows for seamless browsing and swift transactions, thus, making online shopping a breeze. Not only that but on the other end of that transaction, the e-commerce store is capable of being run via a similar device (depending on its scale, of course).

All in all, e-commerce has reshaped how we make money. It transcends borders and enables businesses to reach a global audience. You can sell to customers on the other side of the world and you can do it all while you sleep. Compared to brick-and-mortar stores, e-commerce businesses often have lower overhead costs, which makes them more accessible to entrepreneurs. Plus, e-commerce offers diverse income streams – from selling physical products to digital downloads, dropshipping, and affiliate marketing. It has taken the power of passive income and skyrocketed its abilities.

With dropshipping, for example, you can sell products without the hassle of inventory management. Suppliers handle shipping and you earn a commission. Affiliate marketing is sort of similar in that you can promote other companies' products or services through affiliate links and generate passive income when people make purchases through your referrals. Then you've got digital products and, thanks to marketplaces like Etsy, you can create and sell digital products. The same goes for platforms like Udemy and online courses or Amazon KDP and e-books. If there is a digital product out there, you will find an online marketplace to sell it.

No matter which route you take, data is driving the way e-commerce operates. In this continuous evolution, e-commerce sites use algorithms to provide personalized shopping experiences, thus, increasing customer satisfaction and sales. This is something to keep in mind if you plan on opening your own e-commerce business. If you would rather list products on a marketplace like Amazon, knowing how the algorithms work will be of benefit to you. Just keep in mind that the way these algorithms work is also changing thanks to "voice commerce" via virtual assistants like Alexa and Siri.

When you look at it optimistically, the 24/7 money-making potential of e-commerce, coupled with the rise of passive income streams, will open doors to your financial independence like never before. All you have to do is learn a bit more about how it works and how you can utilize it. At the end of the day, the future is digital.

The Future is Digital: Capitalize on the E-commerce Boom

Welcome to the digital gold rush! Now that you know that the e-commerce industry has experienced unprecedented growth, with no signs of slowing down, here's why you should take notice. A little earlier we discussed how 60% of all internet users now make regular online purchases. However, that's just 60% of current internet users. But if the trajectory that we're on is anything to go by, the data indicates that by 2040, a staggering 95% of *all* purchases will occur online [12]. This monumental shift is a clear indicator of where consumer behavior is headed. A good chunk of those sales is going to go to platforms like Amazon and you can get in on the action. You can create a seller account on Amazon and sell your products via your Amazon storefront. The best part is that Amazon will actually fulfill (deliver) the orders for you if you opt for FBA (Fulfillment By Amazon). With FBA, Amazon handles the heavy lifting, from storage and packaging to shipping and customer service. You focus on sourcing and selling. Additionally, FBA products are often eligible for Amazon Prime, thus, increasing visibility and trust among customers.

What's more, simple products like Dove soap, when sold in bulk, can lead to substantial profits. Now, if you went around knocking on doors and trying to sell people soap out of the boot of your car, you might get a couple of doors slammed in your face. If the price was right, however, someone might buy the lot off you. However, they'd probably be heading to sell them on a platform like eBay or Amazon themselves. As an FBA seller, you're tapping into the power of a trusted platform and it makes selling simple products so much more efficient than trying to do it via your own site, store, or boot.

So, how do you find products to sell?

Well, it's always a good idea to go the wholesale route. This is because sourcing products at wholesale prices is a pivotal step in e-commerce success. It allows you to get products for a fraction of the cost so that you can actually remain competitive when you go to re-sell them.

Next question: how do you find wholesalers?

When in doubt Google it! But also look into attending trade shows or industry events to network with suppliers and discover new products. You can also browse through online marketplaces like Alibaba, Oberlo, and SaleHoo provide access to a vast array of wholesale products. The pros of using platforms like this include the fact that you can access a wide range of products from AliExpress and other suppliers. You can also automate order fulfillment, thus, reducing manual tasks and really upping the passive factor of your income-earning potential. The only drawback is that if you don't pre-order samples, you can't be sure of product quality and reliability from suppliers. We would definitely suggest doing this so that you can become aware of potentially long shipping times for certain products.

In some cases, however, arbitrage can prove to be a profitable option. The simple explanation of what arbitrage is goes a little like this. You walk into Walmart and see that a Scrub Daddy 4-pack is selling for $12. You decide to buy a few boxes and sell them on Amazon, where they're currently selling for $19 per 4-pack. That's how arbitrage works. You find something cheaper in one market and then sell it for more in another market.

But if you're wondering whether or not you could sell your own products on Amazon or via your own website, you would be right. You can sell your handcrafted products as well as white-label products via storefronts like Amazon and Etsy amongst others. White labeling would involve you purchasing physical products from a manufacturer and selling them under your own brand name. In this arrangement, the manufacturer produces generic products that you can then rebrand as if you were the original creator. And before you think that this is some type of scam, most products you consume are white-label. They're all produced in the same factory according to their specific manufacturing processes and then labeled before being sold.

The question of the hour is which of the three is more profitable – wholesale reselling, white label, or arbitrage?

Again, this all depends on what you're hoping to achieve, so we'll give you the pros and cons of each so that you can make an informed decision.

Wholesale Reselling

Pros: Access to a wide range of products, competitive pricing, and potential for long-term relationships with suppliers.

Cons: Intense competition, limited control over product branding, and the need for substantial initial capital.

White Label

Pros: Opportunity to brand products as your own, higher profit margins, and creative control over packaging and marketing.

Cons: Requires product development and branding efforts, potentially higher upfront costs, and greater responsibility for quality control.

Arbitrage

Pros: Quick entry into e-commerce, minimal upfront investment, and the ability to test markets with lower risk.

Cons: Limited scalability, reliance on market fluctuations, and competition from other arbitrage sellers.

No matter which way you decide to go, the e-commerce boom will be your gateway to wealth in the digital age. With statistics pointing toward a future where online sales dominate, there's no better time to embark on your e-commerce journey.

Joining Forces: Accelerate Your Success

We've given you the tip of the iceberg on e-commerce platforms, like Amazon, but we're going to explore how teaming up with e-commerce giants like Amazon, Shopify, Etsy, and other platforms can catapult you toward financial success. First, other than Amazon FBA – where you sell physical products on Amazon – you can also sell designs on Amazon. Let us explain. If you can design cool t-shirts or quirky mugs, you can upload the file to Amazon Merch and Amazon will print and ship those items to your customers. Of course, using Amazon Ads and driving your brand via social media is important but you can still get a few sales without any of that. Nonetheless, if you want to create a substantial income stream out of it, using marketing tools is wise. You can also join the Amazon Associates program to earn commissions by promoting products through affiliate links or review products and get paid while you're at it!

Also, (if you go the FBA route) once you've established yourself as an FBA seller, you can approach popular brands to discuss partnerships. To do this, you need to establish a track record of successful sales and positive customer feedback to gain credibility. Then, approach brands with a clear value proposition that highlights your ability to showcase their products effectively. With time, negotiate exclusive deals or access to limited-edition products, offering a unique selling point to customers.

But it's not all about Amazon and the potential partnerships therein. We also have Shopify, which provides a versatile platform for e-commerce entrepreneurs. With Shopify, you can explore various monetization strategies – from dropshipping to selling digital products. Just like Amazon, Shopify has an official Partners Program and you can join the program to offer your services as a Shopify expert. If you've got an eye for design, you can get on board as a design and development expert. There is also lots of room for anyone who is well-versed in marketing and SEO.

Of course, as with anything that we've discussed, there is always more than meets the eye and if you've heard about storefronts like Shopify, you've likely heard of pre-built stores. In the battle of buying a pre-made Shopify store versus building your own, there are some things to consider:

Buying Pre-Made Stores

Purchasing pre-made Shopify stores can be a shortcut to e-commerce success. However, consider the pros and cons:

Pros: Saves time, includes existing customer base and revenue, and may come with a proven product lineup.

Cons: Higher upfront cost, potential hidden issues with the store's history, and limited customization.

Building Your Own Store

Creating a Shopify store from scratch offers full control but requires more effort:

Pros: Lower initial cost, complete control over branding and products, and the ability to shape the store's direction.

Cons: Time-consuming, steep learning curve, and the need to build a customer base from scratch.

And this is all just the beginning.

Teaming up with e-commerce giants and leveraging social media platforms has never been more accessible. In the final chapters, we're going to explore the power of a personal brand and how you can use nothing more than your experiences to set the stage for your success.

Are you ready?

Then let's leap into our penultimate chapter.

Chapter 9 – Share Your Journey: Monetize Your Expertise Like A Boss

Whether or not you've decided to set up your own e-commerce store, there is something that you can do right now from the comfort of your own home. This next money-making option will have you hustling your way to financial freedom using nothing but your expertise.

Well, with time, you might need a light ring, a better camera (or phone), and other gadgets, but you get the point. You can start sharing your expertise right now with what you have.

More importantly, you can decide whether you want to do this via courses, via one-on-one calls, or via the powerhouse that is YouTube. Ultimately, all you're doing is sharing your expertise and allowing others to capitalize on it. People share everything from how to do an oil change to accounting principles, make-up tutorials, second language basics, and so much more. If there is something that you can teach simply by talking to people or showing them how it's done, there's a market for it.

But not just any markets – massive ones.

People enjoy learning from people. Anyone can Google something but they'd rather have someone walk them through it. This is why there are Facebook groups, Instagram DM pods, and recommendation pages. We're human. We trust other humans to tell us directly how to get something done.

So, if this sounds like something that you can sink your teeth into, let's look at how you can cultivate your personal brand.

Turning Setbacks into Success Stories: Your Personal Brand

In a tech-driven world where algorithms and automation often take center stage, there's an undeniable truth: people buy from people. The human touch, the personal connection, and the authentic stories behind brands and products have become more compelling than ever. But you have to be authentic.

There is simply no other way to create a personal brand.

Plus, nothing ever dies on the internet and followers get really invested in people's stories. If they catch one whiff of a lie, they'll find old content to prove their theory and your online brand will be dead in the water. People get heavily invested in other people because, in a world saturated with advertisements, authenticity is a breath of fresh air. People are drawn to individuals who are real, relatable, and unapologetically themselves.

Simply put, stories matter.

Human stories resonate deeply. Whether it's overcoming challenges, pursuing dreams, or sharing personal experiences, stories are the threads that weave connections between brands and consumers. Moreover, personal branding builds trust and reliability. When customers know the face behind the brand, they feel a stronger bond and are more likely to make repeat purchases.

If there is one cliché saying that we're fans of, it's this: be yourself because everyone else is taken. Authenticity is the cornerstone of personal branding. Share your passions, quirks, and values genuinely. Additionally, be consistent in your messaging, visual identity, and content style. This helps create a strong brand presence and recognition. You want that "Coca-Cola" effect. People should see your color scheme and fonts and automatically know it's a post that you've made. Finally, when people start supporting your content, actively engage with your audience. Respond to comments, participate in discussions, and create a sense of community. This will increase your online following and make you someone who people enjoy listening to.

Speaking of driving your following, here are the steps that you need to take.

Social Media Platforms	Leverage social media platforms like Instagram, Twitter, and TikTok to showcase your personal brand. Share your expertise, experiences, and passions.
Content Creation	Create valuable content that resonates with your target audience. Whether it's blog posts, videos, or podcasts, consistent content keeps your audience engaged.
Collaborations	Collaborate with like-minded individuals or influencers in your niche to expand your reach and tap into their audience.

Table 5: Driving Your Online Following

TikTok is quickly becoming the go-to platform for making money. People spend hours watching videos on TikTok and it seems like the content on that platform has hit the sweet spot. Facebook has us watching too many short reels and YouTube's half-screen setup only gives us the option to rotate our screen to view a video in full. TikTok's videos are just long enough to get people invested and are portrait, making it easier to watch, scroll, and enjoy. Essentially,

TikTok's format allows for engaging, concise content that resonates with users. However, Instagram is on relatively the same level with their reel function and this is why they're number two on the income-earning potential scale.

Now that you understand the basics of building your brand online, you can focus on the art of monetizing social pages. Other than via collaboration and affiliate links, you can monetize your actual videos. YouTube, for example, offers various monetization options, including ad revenue, channel memberships, merchandise shelf integration, and Super Chats during live streams. Similarly, TikTok's Creator Fund allows users to earn money based on video performance, while brand partnerships offer additional income streams. If you are planning on creating an e-commerce store, you can also direct people to your store via your social pages. As our top tip here, try to ensure that your store offers products that are in line with the theme of what you discuss on your page.

But be warned: there is a dark side to developing a personal brand. With visibility comes vulnerability. Online trolls may target you, leaving hurtful comments or engaging in harassment. It's vital to be prepared for this darker side of online fame. Always prioritize your mental health and consider whether this is really for you if you already suffer from poor mental health. Personal branding can be emotionally taxing and it's not the right path for everyone, especially those already struggling with their mental well-being.

If, however, you're determined to make this work, try to develop emotional resilience to deal with online negativity. Reach out to support networks, consider professional help, and know when to step back for self-care. Whatever you do, don't isolate yourself when things go wrong. Get out of the house and immerse yourself in real-world connections. The more you isolate yourself in times of mental struggle, the more likely you are to enter a downward spiral.

Yes, diversify your income by any means necessary...just not at the cost of your sanity. If you find that this is all too much to deal with, you can get behind the lens in another manner: by teaching.

Intersectionality in Entrepreneurship: Teach and Earn

Teaching online has transformed into a powerful avenue for individuals to share their knowledge and earn income. This is because each individual brings a distinct set of experiences, insights, and perspectives to the table – something that we're all appreciating more with each passing day. Diversity enriches the learning environment by offering a wide range of viewpoints and the world is beginning to really wake up to this fact.

Inclusive teaching ensures that learners from various backgrounds, cultures, and walks of life can access and engage with educational content that resonates with them. When there are diverse voices in play, it fosters creative problem-solving. Differing viewpoints can lead to innovative solutions and approaches to challenges.

Knowing this, step into your unique voice. Understand that your life experiences, even the seemingly ordinary ones, hold value. Your unique voice can connect with learners who relate to your journey. To go down this road, identify your areas of expertise and passion. Teaching what you genuinely love and understand best will give you that authentic edge. Take courses of your own and watch YouTube videos (if necessary) to help you develop strong communication skills. This will give you the ability to convey your ideas clearly and engage learners effectively. Ultimately, your teaching style should be a reflection of your personality and not just your expertise. This is because representation in online teaching serves as a source of inspiration. Learners benefit from seeing educators who share similar backgrounds or have faced similar challenges. Additionally, representing underrepresented communities works to challenge stereotypes and foster a more inclusive society. It opens doors for people who might have been discouraged by societal biases.

Here are some of the platforms where you can provide your unique insight and teachings.

1. **Udemy**: Udemy is an online learning platform where you can create and sell courses on virtually any subject.

2. **Skillshare**: Skillshare is a platform for creative professionals to teach and teach through video classes.

3. **Teachable**: Teachable allows you to create and sell online courses, handling everything from course hosting to promotion if you pay for it.

4. **Kajabi**: Kajabi is an all-in-one platform that enables you to create, market, and sell online courses.

5. **Thinkific**: Thinkific lets you easily create and sell online courses, providing tools for course creation, marketing, and student management.

6. **Podia**: Podia is a platform for selling online courses, memberships, and digital downloads with features for building a website and email marketing.

To create inclusive online learning communities, consider the following:

- Ensure that your course content is inclusive, taking into account various learning styles, cultural references, and accessibility needs.

- Encourage interaction and open dialogue among your learners. Create a safe space where different perspectives are respected.

- Be proactive in addressing bias, discrimination, or harassment in your online learning community. Set clear guidelines for respectful behavior.

By embracing diversity and representation, your online teaching can reach a global audience. Learners from around the world can benefit from your knowledge and experiences. As an online educator, you have the potential to create social change by empowering individuals from marginalized communities and underrepresented groups. After all, diversity is the cornerstone of enriching education. For episodic content, there are few places better than YouTube for your content, so let's explore that platform now.

YouTube Titans: The Income Potential of Sharing Your Wisdom

While creating courses and utilizing social media are popular methods of teaching, YouTube offers an equally valuable platform to share wisdom, ideas, and knowledge. This is because YouTube provides free access to a vast library of educational content, making it an inclusive platform for learners worldwide. The fact that video content on YouTube is engaging and memorable makes complex topics easier to understand. Add to this the fact that you can upload long-form content makes this ideal for anyone who wants to break their teachings down into lengthy chapters.

To get started, choose a niche by identifying your area of expertise or passion and then focus your content on that niche. You'll then need to plan your videos carefully and consider your target audience's needs as well as preferences. Steadily invest in decent equipment and editing to ensure your content looks and sounds professional, but don't rush into your investment. You don't need to have a recording studio in your home to make this work.

When the views start rolling in, Google AdSense will give you the power to earn money through ads displayed on your videos. Earnings depend on factors like ad type, viewer location, and engagement, so be sure to go through YouTube's monetization policies to get the lowdown on how this works.

The larger your following, the more monetization avenues available to you, some of which we looked at earlier. These include:

- **YouTube Premium Revenue:** Creators receive a share of revenue from YouTube Premium subscribers who watch their content without ads.

- **Channel Memberships:** Offer channel memberships to viewers who pay a monthly fee for access to exclusive perks and content.

- **Merchandise Shelf:** Sell merchandise related to your channel directly through YouTube.

- **Super Chats:** During live streams, viewers can send monetary donations called Super Chats, which creators receive.

People often get confused as to how YouTube earnings are calculated, but you will be walked through the formulas when you're approved for monetization. Moreover, they also get confused about who can start monetizing their videos. As long as you have 1,000 subscribers and 4,000 watch hours in a 12-month period, you can get monetized. With that in mind, have a look at how monetization is typically calculated.

CPM (Cost Per Mille)	CPM represents the estimated earnings per thousand views and varies based on factors like niche and viewer demographics.
CTR (Click-Through Rate)	CTR measures the percentage of viewers who click on an ad. A higher CTR can lead to increased earnings.
Watch Time	Creators need a minimum threshold of watch time to be eligible for monetization. This is usually around 30 seconds of ad watch time.

Table 6: YouTube Monetization

Now, here are some winning moves for YouTubers. First up, be consistent by regularly dropping videos to keep your viewers coming back for more. And don't sleep on SEO! Use smart keywords and tags so your videos pop up in search results. As with all platforms, be sure to engage with your viewers, reply to comments, and build a real community vibe. Remember that YouTube is a dynamic and impactful platform for teaching. It offers a wide array of opportunities to share wisdom, ideas, and knowledge with a global audience. Monetization on YouTube via ad revenue, channel memberships, and other avenues can provide content creators (just like you) with a means to earn income while doing what they love.

Now let's get into your final chapter on bonus revenue.

Chapter 10 – Bonus Revenue: From Coaching to Ebooks

This is it: your final stop on the road to success. Take some time to think about everything that you've learned this far before we proceed. It will help you adjust to the new ideas that we've led you to. It will also help you digest this chapter more readily.

Why do we say this?

Well, there is a method to the way this book has been laid out. We spent a substantial amount of time toiling over how all of this information would be presented. Finally, we came to the conclusion that, if we had no clue about anything in this book prior to reading, we would want to start with the things that we have most likely already heard of. These are things like investing and credit.

As we said, there's a reason for this and it's as such: getting to grips with the reality that there is more money to be made on TikTok than there is on the stock market can be an insane idea for just about anyone. This is especially true for anyone who has been led to believe that the social media world is simply out of their reach.

But we're here to tell you that once you've done the work of fixing up your credit, investing, and budgeting correctly, there's a myriad of money-making hustles out there for you. With the right approach, these hustles can have you making twice or even three times your current take-home pay.

The first of these hustles involves becoming a coach, mentor, or consultant.

Become a Coach, Mentor, or Consultant: Profit from Your Expertise

For individuals who enjoy connecting with people, sharing your expertise as a Coach, Mentor, or Consultant can pave the way to substantial profits. These roles allow you to provide tailored solutions to individuals or businesses – addressing their specific needs and challenges. By fostering growth and development, you can create lasting, positive changes in your clients' lives. What's awesome here is that the demand for coaching, mentoring, and consulting services is crazy. Not only that but it continues to rise as individuals and businesses seek guidance to achieve their goals.

The cherry on top is the fact that you can carve out a niche in various industries – from career coaching and leadership mentoring to business consulting and personal development. The bonus? High-ticket clients are willing to pay a premium for expert guidance. This means that you can really get into providing just a handful of clients with real value while only working a few hours a week – all the while still earning more than you've ever earned before.

The drawback with mentoring, however, is that some clients may blur the line between professional guidance and personal involvement. This can potentially cause stress and discomfort. Balancing personal time and client commitments is crucial to avoid burnout and maintain a healthy lifestyle. To strike this balance, establish clear expectations and boundaries from the word "go". This is the only way to maintain professionalism and protect your well-being. To make sure that there is no confusion or unrealistic expectations, here are some guidelines to follow:

1. **Create Client Contracts:** Use contracts that outline the scope of your services, confidentiality agreements, and payment terms.

2. **Develop Communication Policies:** Clearly communicate your availability and preferred communication channels to manage client expectations.

3. **Schedule Regular Check-Ins:** Schedule periodic check-ins with clients to evaluate progress and address concerns, reinforcing your commitment to their success.

You can utilize online platforms like LinkedIn, Upwork, or specialized coaching websites to connect with potential clients. Be sure to leverage social media to establish your presence and expertise and remember that platforms like Instagram and YouTube can help you reach a broader audience. Finally, attend industry events, webinars, and conferences to expand your network and connect with potential clients.

In all of this, try not to undervalue your expertise. High-ticket clients are often willing to pay for the unique value you bring to their journey. Instead of devaluing yourself and your services, set competitive rates that reflect your experience and the results you deliver. Believe in the impact of your guidance and the value you provide. Confidence attracts high-ticket clients who trust your abilities. You can also consider offering tiered packages to cater to different client budgets. Remember to be authentic and turn your mess into a message that can inspire others.

Turning Your Mess into a Message: Inspire Others and Earn

Transforming personal challenges into a source of inspiration for others can lead to a lucrative career in public speaking, influencing, or blogging. Sharing your personal struggles and triumphs creates a relatable connection with your audience, thus, inspiring them to overcome their own challenges. As mentioned, authentic storytelling fosters trust and credibility. This allows your audience to connect with your message on a deeper level.

You can turn your adversity into an advantage by transforming life's hardships into a source of motivation. This demonstrates resilience and offers hope to others facing similar obstacles. Here are your avenues for profitable public speaking.

Keynote Speaking	Deliver powerful speeches at conferences, seminars, and corporate events.
Workshops & Seminars	Conduct specialized workshops to share expertise in specific niches.
TED Talks	Share your compelling story or ideas on the global TED stage.
Motivational Speaking	Inspire audiences with motivational speeches that drive positive change.
Speaker Bureaus	Partner with speaker bureaus that connect speakers with events.
Eventbrite	Explore speaking opportunities listed on Eventbrite's event-hosting platform.

If you're going to take this seriously, develop a professional website where you can showcase your expertise and past speaking engagements with time. Create a compelling speaker reel highlighting your best moments on stage as well as a blog that showcases your expertise in your field.

Your blog will become your calling card as it shows others your professional prowess. You don't necessarily need to have your own website to start your blog either. You can start off on Medium, HuffPost, or LinkedIn. All of these platforms accept guest posts and articles so you can start growing a following early on.

If, on the other hand, you want to create your own website, you can go right ahead and do so. Be aware that you'll need to purchase a domain and hosting plan for your website before going ahead and developing a content plan that aligns with your niche and target audience. If you'd like to monetize your blog, you can use some of the tips that we looked at earlier, which include affiliate marketing, sponsored content, and selling digital products.

Top Tips for Building a Blog

1. If you're setting up your own website, be sure to claim that digital piece of property on Bing Webmaster Tools and Google Search Console. If you get started with Google Search Console, you can automatically transfer the data to Bing Webmaster Tools with just one click.

2. Make sure you learn the principles of search engine optimization (SEO) and implement SEO strategies to increase your blog's visibility in search engines.

3. Build an email list to foster a community of loyal readers. You can offer a free e-book in return for people's emails or ask them to subscribe to your newsletter.

The beauty of this model is that turning your "mess" into a message that inspires others is a powerful path to a profitable career in public speaking and blogging. By sharing your authentic story and expertise, you can connect with audiences, drive positive change, and build a thriving brand. Whether you choose to take the stage as a public speaker or share your message through blogging, the potential for financial success is within your reach. Remember that you'll need to share something in order to get your readers to share their email with you – something like an e-book.

Speaking of e-books, let's look at how you can use them to start generating passive income.

E-books as Passive Income: Elevate Your Revenue Game

As we navigate into the final subchapter of your path to unleashing your inner shark, generating passive income through e-books becomes our central focal point. It's an appealing prospect for many aspiring authors and entrepreneurs and for good reason. For starters, e-books require minimal production costs – making them an accessible source of passive income. Once published, e-books can be sold indefinitely without significant additional effort. Additionally, e-books allow you to work on your terms and set your own schedule as well as your own priorities.

First, you need to choose the right e-book genre. If you need to hire someone to help you with this, do it. This is the most important step on your e-book publishing journey – arguably more important than the actual writing phase. Try to find someone – like a book market researcher – to help you identify popular niches with high demand. This will ensure that your e-book caters to a receptive audience. If you can, align your e-book topic with your interests and expertise to maintain enthusiasm throughout the writing process.

Once you've done this, you will need to have your book professionally edited to weed out any potential errors and optimize the book's readability. From there, cover design and formatting are two areas where you can truly make your content shine. While the saying states that we should never judge a book by its cover, that's what most of us do when we head over to Amazon in search of a book. Make your cover artwork pop!

When all of this checks out, you'll also need to market your book. Most people think that you can just publish a book on Amazon KDP or Barnes & Noble and have it sell like hotcakes without any effort. This is completely wrong. Self-publishing is a hugely saturated market right now and if you don't have an existing following or pre-sales, you're going to need to put in the leg work. Up your online presence, get into email marketing, and plan a well-timed book launch. That can include pre-order campaigns, discounts, and giveaways. Consider utilizing Amazon's KDP Select program for promotional opportunities, including Kindle Countdown Deals and free e-book promotions. Here's a fair warning, though: this gives people the ability to read your book in a pay-per-page fashion which can slow your profit-making potential. Using Amazon's advertising sector as well as platforms like BookBub can help curb this issue.

For those of you who are considering this as a passive income vehicle but want to get to grips with the pros and cons, we've got you covered.

PROS	CONS
Control: You have full creative control over your e-book's content, design, and distribution.	Marketing Responsibility: You are solely responsible for marketing and promotion.
Speed: Self-publishing allows for quicker release than traditional publishing.	Quality Assurance: Ensuring a high-quality product requires extra effort.
Higher Royalties: You retain a more significant portion of the earnings compared to traditional publishing.	Limited Distribution: Self-published e-books may not reach as wide an audience as traditionally published books.

Table 7: Pros & Cons of Self-Publishing

But Amazon isn't the only place for you to get published. There are several other platforms that you can use and, once you get the hang of them, you can get books uploaded in a couple of hours. Here they are.

- **Amazon Kindle Direct Publishing (KDP):** Amazon's platform offers a vast audience and a variety of promotional tools.

- **Smashwords:** Smashwords distributes e-books to multiple retailers and allows for a wide distribution reach.

- **Draft2Digital:** This platform simplifies e-book distribution to multiple stores and provides useful marketing features.

- **Lulu:** Lulu offers print-on-demand services in addition to e-book publishing.

- **iBooks Author:** For Apple users, iBooks Author is a tool to create and publish e-books directly to the Apple Bookstore.

Now, let's chat about the legal stuff and how to keep the e-book success train rolling! First up, copyrights. You've got to be on the up and up with copyright laws. Make sure everything in your e-book has the green light legally so you don't end up in any hot water. Remember to place a copyright notice at the beginning of your book and include your ISBN if you have one. Speaking of which, then there's the ISBN decision. It's like giving your e-book its own ID card. Think about whether you want to go for it and give your creation that official stamp. If you use Amazon, you can opt for a free Amazon-issued ISBN but you cannot use it on your books that you'll publish elsewhere. It is a one-time, one-book deal.

Once you're published keep a close eye on sales because numbers don't lie. And hey, don't forget to check out those reader reviews. They're helpful feedback and ideas for making your next e-book even better. It's a learning journey, really. Take what you've learned from the publishing of each e-book, tweak things a bit, and keep going. This self-publishing gig is all about growing, getting better, and expanding your lineup of e-books.

As we wrap up this chapter, understand this: creating passive income through e-books is an achievable endeavor, but it requires careful planning, thorough research, and effective marketing strategies. By selecting the right genre, crafting a quality e-book, and mastering the art of self-publishing, you can unlock a steady stream of income that requires minimal ongoing effort.

We'd like to take a moment to wish you all the best on your journey. With the tools and techniques that you've learned in this book, we have no doubt that you'll make a success of yourself and unleash your inner shark like the boss that you are.

CONCLUSION

As we wrap up this journey together, we hope you're feeling the fire of inspiration. We hope that you're swept up in the thrill of newfound knowledge and the anticipation of what lies ahead. You've walked on a path to financial freedom and we've been right there with you every step of the way. We hope that the guidance that we've offered as well as the insights (and a friendly nudge when you needed it most) will set you up for success.

But it all comes down to how you interpret what we've tried our level best to teach.

Remember when we talked about embracing your inner entrepreneur, that fire within you waiting to be ignited? Well, it's time to fan those flames. Unleash your inner shark – that go-getter, fearless part of you that knows no bounds. When you do, you'll realize that you're not just wading in the shallows. You're swimming in the deep waters of success and it's time to own it!

But success isn't a passive pursuit. You have to be in the ring to actually take part in the fight. So, take action today. What's stopping you? You've learned about financial literacy, the cost of financial ignorance, the power of strong foundations, and the importance of building credit as well as investing wisely. You have everything that you need. Now, it's time to put that knowledge into practice.

Whether you're starting from scratch or fine-tuning your existing financial plan, every step you take today brings you closer to your financial goals. It's about making those small changes, setting clear objectives, and staying the course.

Remember, the world is your oyster. Opportunity abounds and it's waiting for you to seize it. You've explored the rise of e-commerce, the potential of sharing your expertise, the art of using other people's money, and the importance of diversifying your income streams. If this doesn't excite you, we're not sure what else will. So, we want to encourage you to take a minute to think about your next move. Think about what the future looks like – not just for you but for the world. After all, the world is evolving and you're poised to be at the forefront of that change. Grab your chance and hustle on. Be relentless in your pursuit of financial freedom. Keep learning, growing, and adapting.

Remember, this journey doesn't end here. It's a lifelong commitment to securing your financial future and creating a life of abundance. In the grand scheme of things, this book is just the beginning – a stepping stone on your path to financial empowerment.

If no one has told you this lately, we're proud of you. We're so proud of the fact that you went looking for answers and found this book. We're proud of the progress you've made and the determination you've shown. You've tapped into your inner shark and the waters of success are yours to conquer.

Keep swimming, keep hustling, and keep making those dreams a reality.

Conclusion

APPENDIX

- - - - - - - - - - - - - - - - - - -

Appendix A – Recommended Resources: Dive Deeper into the Entrepreneurial World

- - - - - - - - - - - - - - - - - - -

Books:

- *Rich Dad Poor Dad* by Robert Kiyosaki
- *The Total Money Makeover* by Dave Ramsey
- *The Millionaire Next Door* by Thomas J. Stanley and William D. Danko
- *Your Money or Your Life* by Vicki Robin and Joe Dominguez
- *The Richest Man in Babylon* by George S. Clason
- *Think and Grow Rich* by Napoleon Hill
- *The Bogleheads' Guide to Investing* by Taylor Larimore, Mel Lindauer, and Michael LeBoeuf
- *The Wealthy Barber* by David Chilton

Online Courses:

- Coursera – Financial Planning and Management Courses
- Udemy – Investing, Budgeting, and Personal Finance Courses
- Khan Academy – Finance and Capital Markets Courses
- edX – Business and Finance Courses
- Investopedia Academy – Various Financial Courses
- The Balance – Personal Finance Guides and Courses

Websites and Blogs:

- Investopedia – Comprehensive Financial Information
- The Motley Fool – Stock Market and Investment Advice
- NerdWallet – Personal Finance and Investment Guides
- BiggerPockets – Real Estate Investment Resources
- Mr. Money Mustache – Early Retirement and Financial Independence Blog

Financial Tools and Apps:

- Mint – Budgeting and Expense Tracking
- Empower Personal Dashboard – Investment and Wealth Management
- YNAB (You Need A Budget) – Budgeting Software
- Acorns – Automated Investment and Savings
- Robinhood – Commission-Free Stock and ETF Trading
- Wealthfront – Robo-Advisor for Investing

Podcasts:

- *The Dave Ramsey Show* – Personal Finance and Debt Management
- *BiggerPockets Money* – Real Estate and Financial Independence
- *The Clark Howard Podcast* – Consumer Advice and Money-Saving Tips
- *Afford Anything* – Financial Independence and Real Estate
- *The Investing for Beginners Podcast* – Investment Strategies for Beginners

Financial News and Magazines:

- The Wall Street Journal
- Forbes
- Money Magazine
- Barron's
- CNBC

Financial Forums and Communities:

- Reddit Personal Finance (r/personalfinance)
- Bogleheads Forum (bogleheads.org)
- Early Retirement Extreme Forum (earlyretirementextreme.com)

Appendix B – Glossary: Decoding Financial Lingo

1. Angel Investor: A wealthy individual who provides capital to startups in exchange for equity.
2. Arbitrage: Profiting from price differences of the same asset in different markets.
3. Assets: Anything of value that you own, including cash, investments, real estate, and more.
4. Blogger: An individual who regularly writes and publishes content on a blog.
5. Budget: A financial plan that outlines your income and expenses, helping you manage your money.
6. Compound Interest: Earnings on an investment that are reinvested, leading to exponential growth over time.
7. Compound Interest Magic: The phenomenon where reinvested earnings generate even more earnings over time.
8. Credit Score: A numerical representation of your creditworthiness, used by lenders to assess risk.
9. Credit Utilization: The ratio of your credit card balances to your credit limits.
10. Debt: Money borrowed that needs to be repaid, often with interest.
11. Diversification: Spreading investments across various assets to reduce risk.
12. Entrepreneur: Someone who starts and manages a business, often taking financial risks for potential rewards.
13. Fiscal Insurance: Protection against financial losses due to job loss or disability.
14. Financial Independence: Achieving a state where work is optional due to sufficient savings and investments.

15. Financial Literacy: Understanding personal finance concepts and making informed money decisions.

16. Generational Wealth: Building wealth to benefit future generations.

17. Income Streams: Different sources of income, such as salary, investments, or side businesses.

18. Interest Rates: The cost of borrowing money or the return on invested capital.

19. Investment Code: Strategies and principles for successful investing.

20. Investment Portfolio: A collection of investments like stocks, bonds, and real estate.

21. Leverage: Using borrowed money to amplify investment returns.

22. Liabilities: Debts and financial obligations you owe.

23. Millionaire Mindset: A mental attitude and set of beliefs conducive to building wealth.

24. Monetize: Turning a non-income-generating asset or activity into a source of income.

25. Multiple Streams of Income: Earning money from various sources to enhance financial security.

26. Net Worth: The value of your assets minus your liabilities.

27. OPM (Other People's Money): Using borrowed funds to invest or finance projects.

28. Passive Income: Earnings from investments or businesses that require little ongoing effort.

29. Real Estate Investment Trust (REIT): A company that owns, operates, or finances income-producing real estate.

30. Retirement Accounts: Special savings accounts designed to fund retirement, like 401(k)s and IRAs.

31. Risk Tolerance: Your ability and willingness to withstand fluctuations in investment value.

32. Rule Breaker: Developing unconventional income streams to diversify your financial portfolio.

33. Savings: Money set aside for future needs or emergencies.

34. Stock Market: A marketplace where stocks and securities are bought and sold.

35. Tax Deductions: Expenses that reduce taxable income, potentially lowering tax liability.

36. Wealth Building: The process of accumulating assets and investments over time.

37. Yield: The income generated from an investment, often expressed as a percentage.

38. Zero-Based Budget: A budgeting method where every dollar is allocated to a specific expense or savings category.

Appendix C – Worksheet: Crafting Your Personalized Roadmap to Wealth

_ _

Step 1: Define Your Financial Goals

Short-Term Goals (1-2 years):

List your financial objectives that you want to achieve within the next 1-2 years. These can include paying off debt, saving for a vacation, or building an emergency fund.

_____

_____

_____

_____

_____

_____

_____

_____

_____

Medium-Term Goals (3-5 years):

Identify financial milestones you aim to reach in the next 3-5 years, such as buying a home, starting a business, or saving for education.

_____

_____

_____

_____

_____

_____

_____

_____

_____

_____

_____

_____

_____

_____

Long-Term Goals (10+ years):

Envision your financial future and outline long-term objectives like retirement planning, generational wealth, or achieving financial freedom.

_____

_____

_____

_____

_____

_____

_____

_____

_____

_____

_____

_____

_____

_____

Step 2: Assess Your Current Financial Situation

Net Worth Assessment:

Calculate your net worth by subtracting your total liabilities (debts) from your total assets. This provides a snapshot of your current financial health.

_____

_____

_____

_____

_____

_____

_____

_____

_____

_____

_____

_____

_____

_____

Income and Expenses:

Document your monthly income and expenses to understand your spending habits and identify areas for potential savings.

_____

_____

_____

_____

_____

_____

_____

_____

_____

_____

_____

_____

_____

_____

_____

Step 3: Create a Budget

Monthly Budget:

Develop a monthly budget that allocates your income to various expense categories, including necessities (e.g., housing, food), savings, investments, and discretionary spending.

_____

_____

_____

_____

_____

_____

_____

_____

_____

_____

_____

_____

_____

Zero-Based Budgeting:

Implement a zero-based budget, where every dollar has a designated purpose, ensuring that your income is fully utilized toward financial goals.

_____

_____

_____

_____

_____

_____

_____

_____

_____

_____

_____

_____

_____

_____

Step 4: Build Your Emergency Fund

Emergency Fund Goal:

Set a specific target for your emergency fund, typically 3-6 months' worth of living expenses, to provide a financial safety net in case of unexpected events.

_____

_____

_____

_____

Step 5: Pay Off Debt

Debt Inventory:

List all your outstanding debts, including credit card balances, loans, and mortgages.

_____

_____

_____

_____

_____

Debt Repayment Plan:

Develop a strategy for paying off your debts, prioritizing high-interest debts first, and creating a timeline for debt elimination.

_____

_____

_____

_____

_____

_____

_____

_____

_____

_____

_____

_____

_____

_____

Step 6: Save and Invest

Savings Goals:

Determine how much you want to save each month and allocate these savings toward your short-, medium-, and long-term goals.

_____

_____

_____

_____

_____

_____

_____

_____

_____

_____

_____

_____

_____

Investment Strategy:

Choose investment vehicles that align with your goals, risk tolerance, and timeline. Consider diversifying your investments for potential growth.

_____

_____

_____

_____

_____

_____

_____

_____

_____

_____

Step 7: Protect Your Financial Future

Now, it's time to make sure that your financial ducks are in a row.

1. **Insurance Coverage:** Review your insurance policies, including health, life, and disability insurance, to ensure adequate coverage for you and your family.
2. **Estate Planning:** Consider estate planning, including wills, trusts, and powers of attorney, to protect your assets and provide for loved ones.

Step 8: Monitor and Adjust

Make sure to keep track of your progress. Schedule regular reviews of your financial progress to make necessary adjustments to your plan. Then, celebrate your achievements along the way, whether it's paying off a credit card or reaching a savings goal. You can jot them down below.

_____

_____

_____

_____

_____

Step 9: Seek Professional Advice

Consider consulting with a financial advisor or planner for personalized guidance and investment strategies.

Step 10: Stay Committed

Stay dedicated to your financial plan, even when faced with challenges or setbacks. Persistence is key to achieving financial success. Remember that your personalized roadmap to wealth is unique to your financial situation and goals. Periodically revisit and adjust your plan as your circumstances change and as you progress toward financial freedom. Make a declaration to yourself below and come back to it when you need a reminder.

_____

_____

_____

_____

_____

_____

[Signature] _____

Date: _____

LIST OF TABLES & FIGURES

REFERENCES & CITATIONS

1. Sandomir, R. 2003. *Tyson's Bankruptcy Is a Lesson In Ways to Squander a Fortune.* The New York Times. https://www.nytimes.com/2003/08/05/sports/tyson-s-bankruptcy-is-a-lesson-in-ways-to-squander-a-fortune.html

2. The European Commission. 2023. *Poverty And Mindsets: How Poverty And Exclusion Over Generations Affect Aspirations, Hope And Decisions, And How To Address It*. The JRC Report. https://joint-research-centre.ec.europa.eu/system/files/2022-02/1_cassio_presentation.pdf

3. The Consumer Federation of America. 2023. *How Payday Loans Work.* Payday Loans Org. https://paydayloaninfo.org/how-payday-loans-work/#:~:text=The%20average%20loan%20term%20is,from%20390%20to%20780%25%20APR.

4. Sankaran, K. (2004). *Management Studies: An Antidote To Scarcity Mentality.* Business Today, 13(21), 85-85. http://tapmi.informaticsglobal.com/414/1/A26_Sankaran%20Management%20Studies_An%20Antidote%20to%20Scarcity%20Mentality_B%26W.pdf

5. Byrne, D., & Griffitt, W. (1966). *A Developmental Investigation Of The Law Of Attraction.* Journal of Personality and Social Psychology, 4(6), 699. https://psycnet.apa.org/journals/psp/4/6/699/

6. Ramsey Solutions Blog Team. 2023. *How the Debt Snowball Method Works.* Ramsey Solutions. https://www.ramseysolutions.com/debt/how-the-debt-snowball-

method-works#:~:text=The%20debt%20snowball%20method%20
is,the%20next%2Dsmallest%20debt%20payment

7. Rosenblatt, L. 2023. *Amazon Reports Net Loss Of $2.7 Billion For 2022.* The Seattle Times.
https://www.seattletimes.com/business/amazon/amazon-reports
-net-loss-of-2-7-billion-for-2022/#:~:text=In%20a%20year%20m
arked%20by,2022%2C%20the%20company%20reported%20Thurs
day.

8. UNCTAD Reports. 2022. *COVID-19 Boost To E-Commerce Sustained Into 2021, New UNCTAD Figures Show.* UNCTAD.
https://unctad.org/news/covid-19-boost-e-commerce-sustained-
2021-new-unctad-figures-show#:~:text=The%20average%20shar
e%20of%20internet,66%20countries%20with%20statistics%20av
ailable.

9. Macro Trends Team. 2023. *Amazon Revenue 2010-2023.* Macro Trends Online.
https://www.macrotrends.net/stocks/charts/AMZN/amazon/reve
nue#:~:text=Amazon%20annual%20revenue%20for%202020,a%2
037.62%25%20increase%20from%202019.

10. AdvertiseMint Team. 2023. *How Much Does Amazon Make a Day?* AdvertiseMint.
https://www.advertisemint.com/how-much-does-amazon-make-
a-day/#:~:text=Amazon%20rakes%20in%20a%20staggering,minu
te%2C%20and%20%2415%2C000%20every%20second

11. Gillespie, L. 2023. *Survey: 39% Have A Side Hustle, And 44% Believe They'll Always Need One*. Bank Rate.
https://www.bankrate.com/personal-finance/side-hustle-survey/

12. Hernandez, M. 2022. *Worldwide Online Retail Revenues Are Expected To Grow To $5.4 Trillion This Year [...].* The California Business Journal.
https://calbizjournal.com/worldwide-online-retail-revenues-are-

expected-to-grow-to-54-trillion-this-year-thatll-constitute-16-o
f-all-us-retail-spending-by-2040-95-of-purchases-will-occur-onl
ine-according-to-nasdaq-research/#:~:text=to%20Nasdaq%20res
earch.%20%2D-,Worldwide%20online%20retail%20revenues%20a
re%20expected%20to%20grow%20to%20%245.4,online%2C%20a
ccording%20to%20Nasdaq%20research.